TALES OF THE GOLDEN YEARS OF CALIFORNIA OCEAN FISHING

1900-1950

By

Ed Ries

Published by the Friends of the Los Angeles Maritime Museum and the Los Angeles Maritime Museum Research Society

PICTURE CREDITS

Source name is followed by page numbers and positions of illustrations, if needed for clarity.

Wynne Bagley: 86 top left. California Dept. of Fish & Game: 10 center, 12, 13, 27 center right, 29 center left, 31, 34 center, 36 top, 42 bottom, 57, 58 top, 60 bottom left, 66 bottom, 74 top & bottom, 76 bottom right, 80, 81 top, 82, 83 top & bottom, 86 bottom, 87 top & center, 91 bottom right, 93, 109, 114, 115, 117, 118, 125. Chester Doyle: 9, 29 center right, 32 top right & bottom right, 33 top left & bottom left, 36 bottom left, 121. Joe Guion: 29 top left, 32 center, 40, 41, 43 top, 44, 45 top, 49, 52 bottom, 55 bottom left, 62, 67 bottom, 111 center, 116 top. Hollingsworth Collection: 8, 11 bottom, 19 center, 22, 23, 24, 27 top, 28 top left & top right, 29 top right, bottom left, 34 bottom, 35 bottom, 42 top, 47 top, 55 top left & bottom right, 56, 60 bottom right, 95 top, 98, 99, 100 center, 119 top, bottom left, 126. Capt. Harold Huycke: 30, 34 top, 37 top, 54 bottom right, 95 center, 96. C. D. Jones: 38 top. Long Beach Historical Society: 14, 27 left. Los Angeles Maritime Museum, R. Weinstein Col.: 39 bottom. Ernest Marquez: 123 bottom left. Hugh McMillan: 27 bottom, 29 bottom left, 53 top, 61 top, 64 top, 74 center. Marjorie Oefinger Merritt: 51, 52 top & center, 97. Mike Milas: 100 top & bottom. Janet Hall Miles: 25 center & bottom, 26 center, 35 top, 39 top, 53 bottom, 59 bottom, 60 top left, 61 bottom left, 89, 112 top. Miller Family: 26 top & bottom, 58 bottom. James Rowley: 83 center left. Leonard Schipper: 16 center, 17 bottom left, 21 bottom, 28 bottom, 43 bottom, 46 top, 48, 60 top right & center right, 61 bottom right, 66 top, 105, 106 all, 107 all, 112 bottom, 119 bottom right. San Diego Public Library: 79. Maritime Museum Association of San Diego: 37 bottom, 68, 90 top left & right, center right. National Maritime Museum at San Francisco: 38 center. Grey Silva: 101, 102. Norman Taniguchi: 84, 87 bottom, 88, 90 center left, 91 center left & right, bottom right, 103. Phil Tozer: 25 top. K. Urango: 55 top right. Author's Collection: 6, 10 top & bottom, 11 top, 15, 16 top & bottom, 17 top & center, 18, 19 top & bottom, 20, 21 top, 33 center, 45 bottom, 46 bottom, 47 bottom, 50, 53 center, 54 top, bottom left, 59 top, 63, 64 center & bottom, 65, 67 top, 69, 70, 71, 72, 73, 75, 76 top left, 77, 78, 81 bottom, 83 center right, 85, 86 center, 90 bottom, 92, 94, 95 bottom, 104, 108, 110, 111 top & bottom, 113, 116 bottom, 123.

 For more information about this book, write to: FLAMM; Berth 84; San Pedro, CA 90731

Library of Congress Catalog Card Number: 97-60739

Ries, Edward M. 1919-
Tales of the Golden Years of California Ocean Fishing 1900-1950

1. Title 2. Fishing Barges 3. Fishing-California Ocean 4. -History 5. -Tackle 6. -Techniques 7. -Sport 8. -Pier 9. -Commercial 10. -Tuna 11. -boats 12. -Saltwater 13. Trolling

ISBN 0-9657547-0-7 (Hardcover)
0-9657547-1-5 (Softcover)

Printed in the USA.

ACKNOWLEDGMENTS

To all who have helped in the preparation of this book, my sincere appreciation. Especially deserving are those who have so generously shared the family scrapbooks and photo albums that provide rare insight into the fishing past. Among them are Lynn Hollingsworth, Janet Hall Miles, Norman Taniguchi and numerous others listed in the picture credits. I am particularly grateful that I was able to interview and become acquainted with Leonard Schipper, Howard Minor, Mel Shears and Capt. Anthony Mascarenhas, now deceased. Special thanks are also due to Steve Lawson for his invaluable editorial assistance and for keeping my computer in working order, and to Bill Roecker, my onetime editor, for his advice and encouragement. Thanks also goes to companion anglers, skippers and crewmen who help make fishing a major and enjoyable part of my life. Always there for me is my wife, Betty, ready with unwavering support for all my scribbling and endless patience with my fishing obsession over the years. Thanks again!

Ed Ries

FOREWORD

About Ed Ries, Fisherman

Ed Ries began fishing in 1932 and never stopped. Even while in the Navy during World War II, Ed fished the coral reefs of remote islands and atolls. He found new, strange fish there, as much fun to catch as barracuda and yellowtail in Santa Monica Bay. Retired from the Navy in 1966 as a Master Chief Bos'n's Mate, Ries left aircraft carriers and destroyers to captain his own commercial jigboat, and later was a captain of charter sportfishing boats.

Just after WW II Ed attended Chouinard Art Institute in Los Angeles, where he studied fine art and painting. A San Diegan since 1954, he won a house trailer as the second place winner of California's largest salt water tournament, the 1955 Yellowtail Derby. On a 1993 trip to Panama and Costa Rica (...my trip of a lifetime," he called it) aboard a friend's yacht he brought an estimated 750-pound blue marlin to leader on 60-pound line.

Adding to these various careers and achievements, Ries made himself one of the South Coast's most respected writers of sportfishing history, while assembling a large collection of antique photos and documents. A member of the American Society of Marine Artists, Ed's paintings of fishing and life at sea have been purchased, collected and displayed by individuals, museums and corporations.

In 1995 Ed Ries continues to fish twice a week, though arthritis prompts him to stay close to home on day fishing trips. "I hope people will realize how much research has gone into this book," he told me. "I have to write it now or it will be lost forever."

After enjoying many afternoons at the stern rail of the DOLPHIN with Ed, watching and listening as he showed the rest of us how to catch bass and barracuda, yellowtail, halibut and rockfish, I am elated that Ed has finished his book. It belongs in the most-cherished library of every saltwater angler, every lover of fishing lore, everyone who loves the sea and the creatures that live in it. May they all endure, like this book.

Bill Roecker
Oceanside, May 1995

INTRODUCTION

The fishing history of Southern California coastal waters is unique. The following narratives, essays and memoirs deal with the Golden Years, the "good old days" when fish of all kinds were abundant, tackle was crude, and huge catches were routine. Long-forgotten boats, techniques and equipment, both sport and commercial, are described. Contributions of some prime movers in the fishing industry are recorded. Interviews, correspondence and personal experience, backed up by extensive research, form the data base. Published sources are listed in the bibliography and include bulletins and reports of the California Department of Fish and Game, the writings of C. F. Holder and Zane Grey, and items from the old Pacific Fisherman magazine and several newspapers. Much of the material has appeared in South Coast Sportfishing, California Angler and other publications.

Many thanks to those who have donated photos and information. A mere ripple on the surface of California salt water fishing history has been made, but the little I have learned is here.

Much fascinating and historically valuable data remains unrecorded. Aware of great gaps in my account, I hope that someone will make the effort to dig out more facts before they are forever lost. Perhaps other old-timers will fill in some of the blanks before it is too late.

Ed Ries
San Diego, 1996
e-mail: Fishned@AOL.com

"Troller at Work," from a painting by the author.

Contents

Part III THE ABUNDANT FISHES

Part IV FISHING FOR MONEY

Part V PIONEERS AND PERSONALITIES

APPENDIX

Santa Monica Pier, 1928.

Many anglers first sampled saltwater fishing from piers such as this one at Redondo, c. 1926.

Part I
FIRST CASTS
Chapter 1
FISHERMAN'S GENESIS

Ali Baba in the treasure cave could not have been more fascinated. To my intense delight I was admitted to the back room of a bait and tackle store. Sited on Santa Monica Pier between the carousel and the ballroom, the store was the first stop on my introductory saltwater fishing trip in 1930. A kindly clerk opened the counter gate to an inner sanctum where a boy could feast his eyes on hidden wonders.

Pungent odors wafted from the dim interior; mixed aromas of sea creatures alive and dead. A heap of shiny black mussels gave off faint rustling, crackling and popping sounds, pulsing with the movements of starfish, tiny crabs, pile worms and other marine creepers. Wooden tubs held slabs of bonito flesh soaking in brine (a favorite bait for smelt). A row of barrels contained anchovies pickling in coarse salt. Live sand crabs scrabbled in their screened prison.

Stacked boxes of Mustad fish hooks were shelved above bins of lead sinkers. Bundles of bamboo poles filled a corner. Rental rods, marked with identifying blue and orange paint, were racked beside a huge mound of gunny sacks. Hanging overhead were coils of cotton seine twine, hoop nets, grapnels, bait buckets, gaffs and tubes of leader wire. The counter case held reels and wooden spools of linen line, swivels, packs of silkworm gut, snelled hooks and lures of cedar, bone, metal and feathers.

At the outer end of the pier a second store supplied live bait. Overhanging the water in back of the shop was a hoop net about eight feet in diameter. Lowered below the surface, it was chummed with corn meal or ground fish scraps. If there was evidence of baitfish activity the net was quickly cranked up and the catch, if any, transferred to a tank for sale to pier anglers. At night an attractor light dangled over the net.

At the main store my Dad rented a two-guide bamboo pole and sidewinder reel rigged with a "snagline." The latter was a long gut leader with several small, shiny Kirby hooks attached to short droppers. A plated torpedo sinker was tied at the end.

My father knew nothing about sea fishing, and I knew less, but we caught herring (queenfish), horse sardines and jacksmelt in quantity. Emulating other snaggers, we levered our rod up and down over the top railing until something hit the shiny hooks. Elated with our catch of eight to ten inchers, we proudly cleaned and ate the bony, oily little critters.

After my first snagline success I was so badly bitten by the fishing bug that I thought of little else. When I could not actually be fishing I read about it, drew pictures of it, and dreamed about it day and night. My imagination was wildly stimulated by the fishing tales of Zane Grey and C. F. Holder. I read every word of the massive tomes written by Jordan and Evermann, the biologists who first described West Coast fishes. From them I learned the family classifications and Latin names of all the common species.

The perch picker.

So obsessed was I with everything related to fishing that countless hours were spent mooning over tackle displays and in browsing through the many catalogs I received in the mail.

When at last I was permitted to travel to the pier by myself I was operating on an allowance of 25 cents a week. After considerable begging my Dad was persuaded to let me borrow his rarely used trout tackle.

On my first solo trip I traipsed up and down the pier in an agony of indecision over where to drop my line. After inspecting everyone's catch I squeezed between a pair of successful halibut anglers. A pyramid sinker was tied to the end of my enamelled silk fly-casting line and a snelled salmon egg hook was attached a few inches above the weight. Collecting a piece of the reject bait that littered the planks, I buried the tiny hook in a sun-dried anchovy and plopped it in.

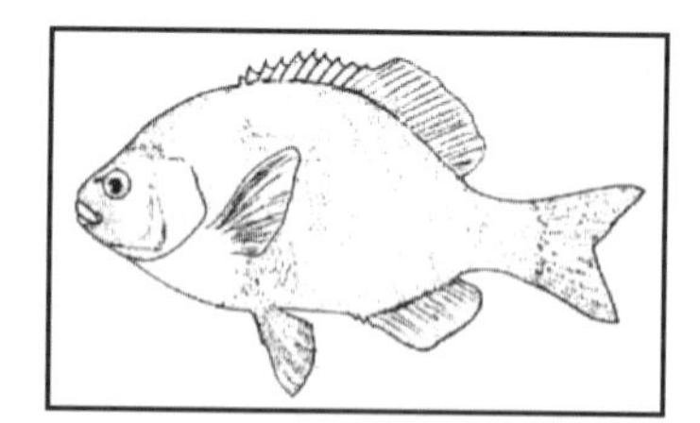

Buttermouth perch.

Halibut continued to be caught but I got nary a nibble. Disappointed but not discouraged, on my next trip I brought along a coffee can to hold a few live anchovies. Still no halibut for me. A queenfish and a small shovelnose shark were all I could manage. The latter caused a little stomach flutter before it surfaced. I was sure I had at last hooked a prized halibut. The results on my next few ventures were no better and I sought another way to catch fish.

Aiming at less prestigious prey, I switched to mussel bait. A bit of shellfish rind on a salmon egg hook was just right for small-mouthed perch. Shiner, walleye, and black surfperch made up the bulk of my newly increased catch, augmented occasionally by a bonus sargo (usually called "Chinese croaker" by pier fishermen).

Oblivious to dead bait, bird droppings and splinters I crouched or lay full length at the edge of the pier deck, tending my handline. Fishing ceased at nightfall, eight or ten hours later. Filthy, tired and famished, I toted my flour sack of perch up the hill to the trolley stop.

At the time, 1931, we lived in the Hollywood area and my fishing forays were made on the big red cars of the Pacific Electric Railway. To prevent offense to other passengers, the conductors usually made me and my odorous sack of fish ride in the windy vestibule at the back of the car. My mother was kind enough to cook the catch, but cleaning fish was a skill I had to master quickly in order to maintain parental approval of my more frequent trips.

For my 1932 Christmas gift I received an inexpensive jointed rod of yellow cane, a sidewinder reel and a tin tackle box. Crude as the new equipment was it helped increase my catches. In addition to perch and tomcod, I took bonito, mackerel and an occasional barracuda or halibut.

In June of 1933 we moved back to Santa Monica and my fishing expeditions shifted from the occasional to the constant. We resided at the Lido Apartments at 4th and Broadway, a few minutes' walk from the pier. Nearly every day that wonderful summer I was up and out at dawn. At the pier I wallowed in fishing until hunger and fatigue finally drove me home. So obsessed was I that my parents began to fear for my sanity and my father declared that I was little better than a "wharf rat." Every type of fishing available locally from pier, boat, barge or beach was sampled.

NIGHT OF THE CROAKERS

Surf fish were exceptionally abundant at Santa Monica that year. On an evening when I was returning from a day of pier fishing for perch two experienced anglers were casting their lines into forming swells near the shore and coming out with spotfin croakers two at a time. Already late for supper and facing a sure bawling out from my parents, I nevertheless paused to watch the action. What red-blooded young fishing fanatic could resist the temptation?

My clumsy sidewinder reel and bamboo rod were unlimbered in a moment. Tiny number 12 hooks suitable for perch were already rigged and a few mussels had been saved for the next outing. Pinning a few chunks of shellfish rind on the miniature hooks, I plunked my offering into the drink a few yards from the other fishermen. A turn of line was taken around a reel knob and the rod propped

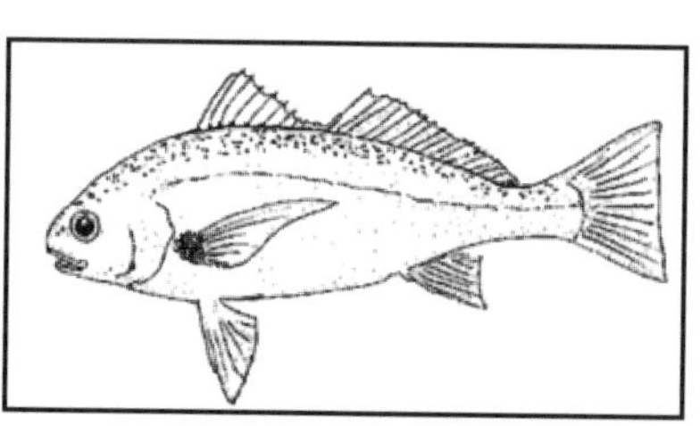

Spotfin croaker.

between upper and lower railings. The butt was wedged under one of the benches lining the pier.

Putting the tackle aside at that moment was foolish, but I rushed to watch the other anglers. One had lowered a hoop net into which his partner was struggling to maneuver a huge croaker. The fish was one of those outsized spotfins of a distinct golden hue that led some sportsmen to regard them as a separate species. The giant fish, a five-pounder at least, escaped. It was then I was alerted by the clatter of my own rod lashing at bench and rail.

Thrilled and excited, I began cranking against strong resistance. Getting the proper lift was difficult with the rod between the railings. Two large croakers were on my line. When I attempted to wind them up to the pier deck their thrashing and flopping proved too much for the small hooks. Both fish twisted loose and dropped back into the sea.

Swallowing my disappointment, I rebaited and cast anew and was rewarded with instant fish as hungry croakers snapped the bait. Again and again I lost the larger fish, but succeeded in landing a sample of the smaller sizes.

A serendipity of cabezon.

All track of time was lost. It was not surprising that my father had fire in his eyes when he arrived on the scene. Burning under a severe tongue-lashing, I wound in my line with a final catch. At the same moment the neighboring anglers bounced a pair of sizeable croakers over the rail. Dad's tirade dwindled and after a moment's hesitation, he too, succumbed to the spell of wide-open fishing. Minutes later he was hauling in a spotfin on my crude rig and no more was said about my tardiness.

So vast was the school of croakers that on the back of each swell hundreds could be seen, their sides flashing and glinting in the glow from pier lamps. The Night of the Croakers remains one of the most vivid of my fishing memories.

CABEZON CRAWL

Always accessible from the pier were the perch which continued to be targeted when more desirable species were unavailable. If the light was right and the sea calm, the ghostly shapes of monster rubberlip and pile perch could be discerned gliding serenely through the centerline stands of pilings. The wary creatures could sometimes be enticed away to bite on small rock or sand crabs but they seemed to prefer hanging around the interior pier structure.

Takeoff for my cabezon crawl was from the landing ramp.

Determined to pursue big perch where they lived, I learned to climb about under the pier deck, scooching along the four-by twelve timber stringers that tied the pilings together. By getting close to the center pilings I could fish areas inaccessible from the deck edges above. Takeoff was from the boat landing ladder and a little monkey-work would put me where I could creep along the stringers. Slung over my shoulder was a flour sack secured by a cord tied to the open corners.

Armed with a handline wound on a stick and a can of soft-shelled crabs, I would crawl to a cluster of interior pilings and drop my bait as close to the crusting barnacles as possible. Not many perch were captured but there was a serendipity. Each wooden piling had a thick collar of mussels creating a mushroom-like overhang. Under the overhangs lurked an unseen and unexploited population of cabezon eager to bite. Six or seven of the smooth-skinned fish was the usual reward for a couple hours effort on the stringers.

My Mother welcomed edible fish to add to our Depression menu, but she balked at the green-fleshed cabezon until I persuaded her to fry a batch. Thereafter the tasty critters were always acceptable.

Access to my secret cabezon cache was cut off when a lower pier deck was expanded to accommodate a cafe, fuel dock, boat storage and other fixtures.

Persistent effort overcame my lack of skill and eventually enough fish were caught and sold to replace my sidewinder with a cheap conventional "knuckle buster" reel. With it my casting and fish-handling were further improved. Boat fishing began to supplant pier fishing.

Larger catches on the boats led to increased earnings and I was able to buy and wrap a Calcutta rod. With better tackle I could earn a place among the "kid commercials." I felt I had arrived as a savvy fisherman.

BAIT HAULER

At age 15, in the summer of 1934, I was fishing six days a week on Santa Monica's Morris boats. In order to cut my expenses, I begged manager Jack Duggan to let me help with the bait catching in return for free rides. Duggan agreed as extra hands were welcome in those days of labor intensive methods.

At 0530, along with the regular bait haulers, I boarded the 38-foot LARK. The skipper had rowed to the mooring in a skiff lowered from the pier derrick. As the boat moved at a slow cruise, two men stacked the net on the port side, ready for setting. The others stood at the bow or atop the cabin trunk looking for signs of bait fish. There were no electronic aids; it was all done by eyesight.

"Let 'er go!

Anchovies were usually located by flips, tiny splashes like raindrops dotting the calm early morning sea. Sometimes they were revealed by the flashing of their gill plates as they fed, or by a dark color spot in the water. Diving pelicans were another clue. Sardines made a sort of "breeze."

When the boat was positioned for a set the skipper would holler, "Let 'er go!" The buoyed end of the net would be tossed overboard as the boat circled rapidly to starboard. If all went well the bait school would be surrounded as the net payed out. The buoy would be picked up and the anchor dropped. Hard, back-straining work then commenced. With two or three men to a side, both wings of the net were pulled aboard together. As a novice, I was allowed to pull only webbing. Later I learned to haul and stack corks and leadline so that they would deploy properly on the next set.

If the haul was successful, the bait would be concentrated in the fine-meshed sack at the center of the net. From there it could be scooped into the tanks of waiting sportboats. If the bait escaped, it was a "water haul." Eight or ten sets were sometimes made before sufficient bait was obtained. If a school could not be located by sight it was customary to make a blind haul just outside the surf. Herring (queenfish) and tomcod (white croaker), usually present in the shallows, were furnished to the waiting boats in lieu of anchovies.

As the last boat was baiting out alongside I would climb aboard for the fishing. By the time the trip ended and my catch was sold I had put in a very long day.

Halibut, sea trout, sargo, croaker and butterfish were often captured along with the bait, especially in shallow water sets. "Preo" was the bait crew's slang for the side money earned by culling and sale of the larger specimens.

Completing the bait haul with a hand-pulled lampara net.

Numbers of non-bait fish were often mixed with the bait and scooped into sportboat tanks. Passengers were usually allowed to dip their own bait and would poke about in the bottom of the tank for the choicer pieces. Crewmen coined the word "plungers" to describe the bait tank diggers and eventually it became a sort of generic term for all sportboat anglers.

Cotton twine then used in nets rotted and tore easily. It was necessary to wash the slime and scales from the sack of the net when hauling was finished. Countless man hours were expended patching tears and when major rips occurred the net had to be brought ashore and stretched out on a flat surface. As a preservative, the net was stacked in a huge vat and boiled with tanbark (oak chips). The webbing was colored a rich brown by the process.

In the mid 'twenties alert owners began furnishing bait nets for their sportfishing boats. Eventually one boat would concentrate on furnishing bait for a number of headboats operating from the same location. As sportfishing grew in importance, specialized bait-catching businesses developed. In San Diego, sardines were caged in large floating pens (receivers), increasing live bait availability. In Los Angeles Harbor, anchovies were attracted and caught at night with the aid of bright lights shining from anchored skiffs.

With the introduction of stronger, non-rotting synthetic webbing in the 1960s, larger nets handled by mechanical means were feasible. Spotted by airplane, bait can now be wrapped with huge pursable drum seines and siphoned aboard built-for-the-purpose boats holding a thousand scoops. Such modern high-tech methods make it practicable to round up bait far offshore, an impossibility with the old hand-pulled cotton nets.

LOOPING THE SNAKES

Shown in the photo on the next page is a typical 1936 catch from local live bait boats. It was taken on the Santa Monica Pier in front of the Galley Cafe with the La Monica Ballroom in the background. The lads in the picture were friends and contemporaries of mine from 16 to 18 years of age. On the left is Tom Heany, a fellow lightweight footballer at Santa Monica

High and a tough player. The second kid is looking down and unidentifiable. Third from the left is Pete Breceda, another Samohi footballer. He later became a police officer. Always popular with the girls, the curly-haired fellow on the right is Clancy Bevington. He later piloted the little taxi boat that serviced vessels moored in the so-called yacht harbor. The make of the auto is unknown, but many such 1920s models were still in use. Large catches were sometimes loaded into our Model-T Fords or other ancient vehicles and hauled into the hinterlands of L.A. There the fish were easier to dispose of, sometimes to restaurants or "Mom & Pop" markets.

The snakes are strung on a rope, often preferred to the sacks that caused barracuda to curl up like horseshoes. The drawback of stringing was that some fish were bound to drag and pick up splinters and abrasions from rough pier planks. Besides a dandy haul of barries, several yellowtail were taken and a sizeable halibut lies on the planks. No-limit slaughters were common at every fishing port on the South Coast sixty years ago. In the slang of the day, we "looped 'em" or "knocked 'em dead."

As the fish are strung together it is likely that the fishing buddies have formed a "corp" (for corporation), a pooling of the take by two or more anglers. Handling, transporting and selling a big catch was easier when the work was shared. Profits, if any, were split evenly by the partners.

Barracuda are not highly esteemed as food today, but were popular table fare then. The fish would be peddled wherever possible, some perhaps to the gents in the straw hats.

The barracuda brought about 25 cents each, the yellows maybe 50 cents and the halibut 75 cents, or a bit more. We sometimes took as little as 10 cents apiece for the snakes if nightfall found us with fish still unsold. On such days in the Depression years I often made more money than my father.

Recovering the cost of the boat fare for the next trip was imperative. Busted only once for selling fish without a license, I was let off with a warning by the arresting officer. My ragged, smelly appearance and woeful look may have convinced him that I was not a real criminal type.

Looping the snakes.

In a 1921 photo this gent shows off a nice bluefin tuna. His reel has a Williams drag. The lure is described on page 12. The rod socket resembles a soup can.

Part II
FISHING WITH LINEN, WOOD AND WIRE
Chapter 2
TACKLE

RATTLESNAKE OR FISHING REEL?

Bet you think "sidewinder" as an ocean fishing term refers to some kind of lure, a live rattlesnake bait (if your imagination is active) or some such? Not so! My first fishing reel was a sidewinder, which with a crude rod and tin tackle box was my 1932 Christmas gift. It was a simple single action device similar to a fly reel, but with the seat at the end of the axle post so that it mounted flat to the rod. The perforated side plates were about seven inches in diameter and the pillars were about an inch wide. Two opposing wooden knobs served for handles. It was always awkward to use and its axle and brass bushing required frequent oiling to prevent freeze-up.

Called a Pflueger "Taxie," this plated brass contraption was originally designed to hold wire line used in deep trolling for lake trout. As a cheap substitute for conventional ocean reels, it was used mostly for pier fishing. Although only one step removed from a handline, it was often provided on rent rods by pier bait shops and occasionally it appeared on boats.

Wooden sidewinders for salt water fishing were in use as far back as 1897. With spool diameters of 5 to 8 inches, they were made of selected maple wood. In 1900 the smallest size sold for as little as 20 cents. For three dollars, one could buy a *de luxe* 7-inch mahogany model with a ball bearing bushing.

To get any vertical winding action, as with conventional reels, it was necessary to rotate the rod ninety degrees. Line tension on the sides of the guides, rather than on the bottom, would cause a sideways set in the bamboo. With no drag and no gears, the sidewinder was not suited for heavy fishing. Finger grip on the knobs was all one had to overcome fish resistance. I've never caught a lake trout but can't imagine them putting up much fight if anglers were able to crank them in with a sidewinder. Perhaps, if one could maintain a grip on the knobs, it didn't take long for the weight of the wire line to exhaust the fish.

I could get the weight going in a nice arc...

On one occasion I hooked a very large barracuda from the Santa Monica pier and was unable to wind it up the 20 or so feet to the deck. The scooter thrashed about for agonizing minutes before a kindly bystander seized the other reel knob and helped me winch up the log.

Casting with such a crude device would seem out of the question, yet I learned to do it. After days and days of practice there came a time when I could fling a six ounce pyramid sinker a respectable distance with an underhand cast.

Perched on the middle pipe of the pier railing and leaning far over, I could get the weight going in a nice arc. If my timing was good and the line didn't wrap a stringer, the lead would splash 40 or 50 feet away from the pier. With the line secured by a turn around a handle, the rod could be propped against the rail while waiting for action.

On one of my first ventures aboard a live bait boat, the skipper spotted my sidewinder and shunted me to the bow. It was a wise decision as the hefty mackerel and barries I hooked were nearly unmanageable with my rig. Frustrated by tangles and wraps around the anchor line, I also endured some sarcastic ragging by neighboring anglers. On succeeding boat trips I used a handline, which was permitted then, until I caught and peddled enough fish to earn the price of a conventional "knuckle buster" reel.

For all its drawbacks as a fish winch a sidewinder had three things going for it: (1) simple, one screw mechanism for easy maintenance; (2) open frame design allowed line drying right on the reel; (3) they were inexpensive which was an important factor in the Depression years.

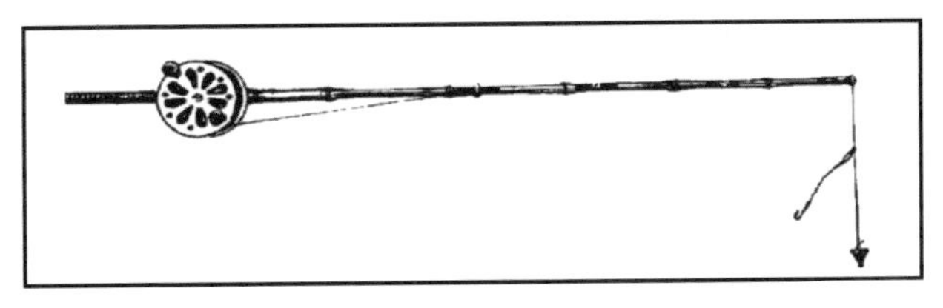

The sidewinder rig.

Typical "knuckle buster" reel with leather thumb drag.

As a way to coil and store fishing line, sidewinders had a place. They handled the usual catches of perch, croakers and small halibut well enough. They filled a minor need at the time, but I don't think I've seen a sidewinder for over fifty years. They are not likely to be missed.

BAMBOO AND KNUCKLE BUSTERS

When California rod and reel fishing began a century ago, most tackle was manufactured on the East Coast. Reels were designed primarily for surfcasting and bottom fishing. A few models were made for tarpon, then the largest game fish pursued with sporting gear.

Nickel, bronze and hard rubber were the materials used on better quality reels. Strongly built to handle the expansion and contraction of linen lines, they were clumsily heavy compared to modern reels. Cheap reels were simply plated brass. Spinning tackle was unknown until after World War II.

In 1913 William Boschen took the first ever broadbill swordfish on rod and reel. Using a new reel with an internal braking system of his own design , he made tackle history. After two years of tinkering, Boschen had reelsmith Julius vom Hofe do the machine work on his invention. On his next trip to Catalina he collaborated with Joe Coxe to perfect the design. As a result of his swordfish catch, all skeptics were silenced. His basic friction clutch drag system is still used today.

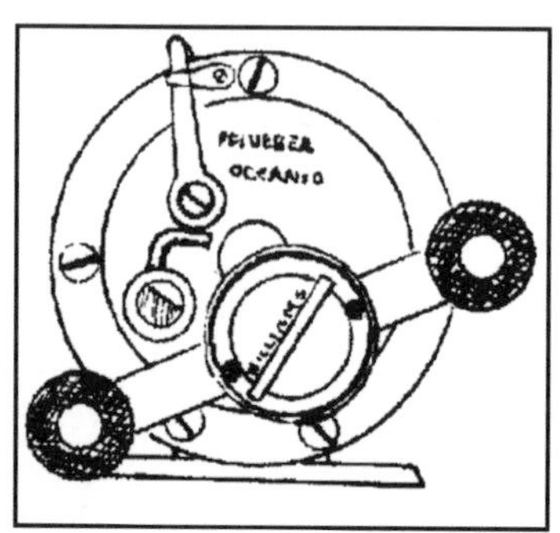

Williams drag.

Competing with the Boschen-Coxe internal brale was the Williams external drag. Sold as a separate kit, it could be adapted to several types of Pfluefer reels. The mechanism was part of the handle, but there was no star wheel. Brake pressure was applied by twisting a raised ridge of metal. It must have been difficult when fingers were slimy and wet. There was also an external spring-loaded detent arrangement that could be set to prevent the handle from spinning backwards when the reel was in gear. The whole thing was awkward, but better than mere thumb pressure, then the usual method of controlling running fish. A similar mechanism even more clumsy and short-lived was the Rabbeth handle drag.

A later model of the Williams drag equipped with a stubby star wheel was standard on the "Templar" reel, originally developed for tarpon fishing, but also popular for heavy duty on the West Coast. Updated Pflueger reels had internal drags.

Pflueger was a big name in mass-produced reels during the 'teens and 'twenties. The "Ohio" and "Capitol" models are examples. In 1935 an "Ohio" was my first star drag reel, but I had to peddle a lot of fish to accumulate the $6.50 cost. Pflueger also advertised a dragless reel with free spool, known as the "Golden West," for $3.50. Ocean City had the similar "Brigantine" at $4, but the star drag "Bay City" matched the "Ohio" price.

Montague turned out a multitude of reels under house brands. Ocean City, Bronson-Coxe and Meisselbach all built salt water reels. The latter made the "Good Luck" wooden sidewinder, among others. Reels long out of production include the Shakespeare "Jupiter," the Four Brothers "SUMCO," Western Auto Supply's "WASCO" and Ocean City's "Farcast."

Long Calcutta rods decorated with turkshead knots were standard.

Affluent fishermen favored the classic reels of the vom Hofe brothers. In the 'thirties, Arthur Kovalovsky built large capacity custom reels for Zane Grey and other big-game anglers. Production of Penn reels began in 1931 and they were rapidly gaining a major share of the market when the war began. Their most popular model was the sturdy "Long Beach."

Many varieties of so-called boat rods were offered by Eastern manufacturers. Most were short, stiff and club-like, more suitable for hauling cod and pollock off the bottom than flylining anchovies and sardines.

Surf rods had long wooden "spring butts," one set of over-and-under guides and a reversible tip. Brass ferrules on the detachable section of the pole were difficult to separate. The Montague City Rod & Reel Co. of Brooklyn, Mass produced thousands of split bamboo rods, including many sold under house brands. They featured ribbed wooden butts and foregrips, one set of double guides halfway up the shaft, and a stirrup tip. Heavy duty rods were fashioned from hickory, greenheart and other resilient woods.

Salt water rods of tubular steel were introduced by the Gephart Mfg. Co. in 1937. None of the twelve models was a success in California. A light tackle rig had a 14-inch butt, a five-foot tip, weighed six ounces and sold for $15. Ten years later, another metal rod was on the market. Warren Products of Los Angeles advertised beryllium-copper alloy rods obtainable in lengths to 8½ feet. Their high cost of $43 to $75 in 1947 ruled out wide popularity, but I saw a number of them in use before fiberglass took over.

When live bait fishing from boats became available to fishermen of modest means, a sort of standard rod was developed. Californians, accustomed to fishing with bamboo jackpoles from piers and barges, found it logical to add a few guides and a reel to the long sticks. Many anglers wrapped their own rods of Tonkin and Calcutta cane.

Guides were mounted on the cane poles with Kingston, a heavy cotton thread. It was much cheaper and easier to wrap than the silk on factory rods or the slippery nylon used today. Guides were placed on top of nodes, or joints, which were fairly smooth on Calcutta sticks. Reinforcing wraps between nodes were usually added and solid-wrapped rods were common. The butt section was covered by heavy cord and finished off with turkshead knots for decoration. Five coats of marine spar varnish were applied to finish the job. Skeleton reel seats were available or reels could be secured with simple hose clamps.

Anglers today would find the cane rods excessively long, often reaching 12 feet or more. The extra length made it a little easier to lob an anchovy or sardine away from the boat. Long rods were also advantageous for pier, surf and barge fishing, pastimes then more commonplace.

A heavy strain could be put on tackle and fish with 36-pound test line and wire leaders.

With use, bamboo rods acquired a permanent bend or set, and the approved way to remove it was to hang the rod by the tip with a weight attached to the butt. Putting the tip on the ground and bending backward against the set was a method sometimes used by those who fished daily. Rods subjected to that treatment soon became soft and lost their spring.

VEGETABLE LINES

Be thankful for modern technology. If you began fishing during the past 40 years you have used only synthetic lines of nylon or Dacron. In the Old Days twisted vegetable fiber lines were standard and the problems we had with them far exceeded any you will ever have with today's monofilament.

Casting aids.

Cuttyhunk was a sort of generic name for linen lines. Made of flax, they were graded according to the number of threads in multiples of three. The wet breaking strength was approximately three pounds per thread. Three to 39-thread sizes were available, but 12-thread, or 36 pound test, was favored for all-around fishing. Most fish up to eight or ten pounds were bounced, so a stout line was needed. Nine-thread was the next most popular and larger sizes were for big-game fishing. Fifteen-thread was considered medium and 21-thread was standard for heavy tackle. For live bait fishing, green-dyed line was generally preferred over the natural off-white color. It was usually sold on 50-yard connected wooden spools.

Line drier.

Ashaway, Cortland, Gladding and Sunset were well-known manufacturers, but every major tackle store had its own house brand. Mermaid, Rain Beau and Catalina Red Thread were popular locally. Barbour's Linen was furry and loosely laid, but less expensive.

Fiber lines were so fragile and easily ruined that preservation was a major concern. A single tiny spot of blood, rust or slime could rot through a line almost overnight. If a reel was put away with wet line spooled, mildew was sure to sprout. Prolonged exposure to sunlight was also damaging. To aid drying, wet lines were wound off on special open-frame wooden reels or loosely coiled on a spread newspaper and sprinkled with salt.

Glass and agate-ringed guides were an attempt at reducing groove-cutting line friction. In the surf, fiber lines absorbed fine sand that accelerated wear on guides and thumbs alike. A leather pad hinged to the back crossbar was fitted on many reels to protect the thumb while pressure was applied in casting or playing a fish. Another thumb brake

1934 ad for Gladding lines.

was a hinged hardwood bar pressed to the shoulder of the spool flange. When casting a fine spray flew from the water-saturated lines.

Reel spools were stoutly built to handle the swelling of wetted lines. Overcoming spool inertia was possible only with heavy baits. Other methods were developed to cast a small live bait and keep it near the surface. A ball of red sponge rubber about two inches in diameter was rigged as a slider above a three-foot wire leader. A short length of broomstick with a screw eye in either end was another casting aid, as was a net cork with a sinker wedged in the center hole.

A few sharp anglers tried to lighten up their gear by fishing with the braided silk casting lines made for tossing plugs at freshwater bass. I saw this mostly at Catalina where line-shy bluefin tuna and yellowtail frustrated fishermen as they swarmed around the boat, easily visible in the clear water, but hard to hook on pinhead bait. With the thin, black silk line, a fine-gauge wire leader and a #8 hook it was sometimes possible to get enough natural action out of a pinhead anchovy to entice a tuna bite. The excessive fragility and high cost of silk lines precluded their wider use.

So, anglers, give three cheers for nylon monofilament and the DuPont Company which pioneered in its manufacture and use for fishline. Next time you are picking out a backlash stay cool and be thankful that chemistry has given you smooth, limp, transparent, mono lines. They are the deadliest fish catchers yet invented in three thousand years of recorded fishing effort. Yet another huge advance in tackle technology has come with introduction of the new gel-spun polyethylene lines featuring low stretch and high strength in small diameters.

GUTS FOR LEADERS

Silkworm gut was the most transparent and flexible terminal tackle available in the time before nylon was invented, but it was definitely not as satisfactory in any category as monofilament. When you consider that it was made from a worm's insides—actually the material they used to spin their cocoons—it is not surprising that it left something to be desired as a fishing aid. For lack of anything better it served that purpose for at least 200 years, mostly for fooling finicky freshwater species. In spite of its drawbacks it was as superior to Isaac Walton's horsehair leaders as modern mono is to gut itself.

The best Spanish gut used for trout fishing was not available in high tests or long lengths. For ocean fishing the Japanese manufactured type was preferred. Built up of silk yarn fixed with glue and seaweed extracts, it was dyed blue or green.

A gut leader was usually coiled in loops small enough to fit a pocket. It quickly took a set and retained a springy spiral shape that was difficult to eliminate. Hard stroking with a piece of rubber tire inner tubing held between thumb and forefinger helped a little, but long soaking was needed before it attained any real degree of limpness. Only semi-transparent compared to the stuff used for trout, it was at least more flexible than wire.

Gut was used in light duty salt water fishing from piers and for bass and halibut from boats. Long-shanked eyeless hooks snelled to short gut leaders were sold in packages of six. They were manufactured by wrapping the gut to the hook shank with red silk thread and coating the splice with varnish. Hooks of this type were suitable only for the likes of perch, jacksmelt and tomcod.

Gut was the leader material on bait-catching rigs similar to those used today for small mackerel and squid. The multiple tiny feathered hooks were referred to by the venerable Holder as "Japanese flies" and he declared them very effective for snagging sardines.

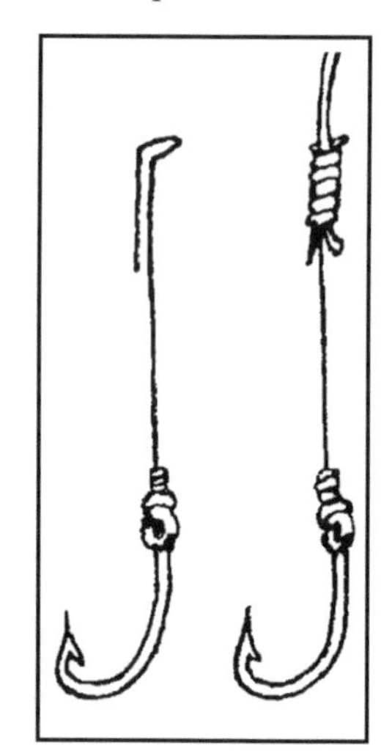

Rig for gut-and-wire combination leader.

Some anglers preferred gut to wire for almost any purpose. If toothy critters like barracuda were biting, a combination leader was rigged. They could be bought in tackle shops, but I quickly learned to make my own. A piece of stainless steel leader wire about four inches long with a 2/0 hook attached was prepared. With needle-nose pliers the free end of the wire was doubled and bent to form a turned down eye, as shown in the drawing. A two or three foot length of well-soaked gut in 30 pound test was then tied to the wire with a return knot. The knot was drawn tight over the doubled part of the wire and through the eye, eliminating the need for the little bronze ring usually used to prevent wire cutting gut. It was a popular arrangement for all-around live bait fishing, but not really suitable for strong fish such as yellowtail and tuna.

Short, plastic-coated wire leaders for the end of monofilament line are available today, but I never use them--spooky fish will usually shy away from anything so visible.

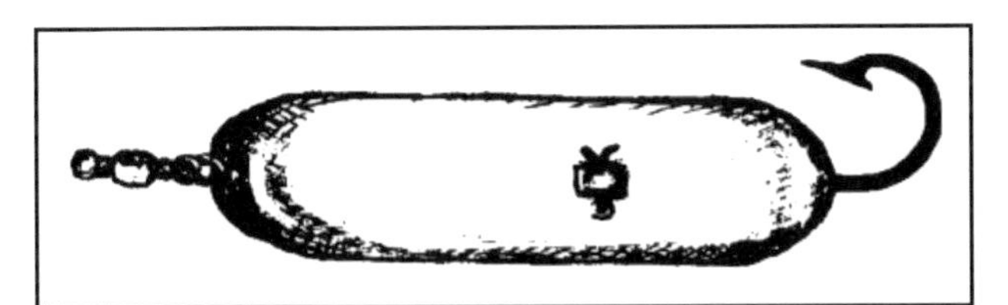

Wilson spoon.

GETTING WIRED

Several types of wire leaders were used for heavy duty salt water fishing. High-carbon steel, commonly called piano wire, came in either plain, tinned or stainless single strands. The plain and tinned varieties had high tensile strength, but rusted so fast that they were good for only one day of fishing. Stainless steel gradually prevailed and was available in bright or blued finish. Malin's "Wilstabrite," the predominant brand, came in packaged coils or in cut lengths of four and eight feet.

Sizes favored for live bait fishing were #2 to #8, from 27 to 86 pounds breaking strain. The lightest wire was seldom used unless targeting bluefin tuna with small bait. Commercial trollers used #8 and #10 for barracuda, etc. while #12 or #14 was usual for albacore.

Twisted multiple strand wire leaders were used for active, heavyweight fish such as marlin and black seabass, and to a lesser extent for live bait fishing. The twisted wire was not easy to manipulate when securing to hooks and swivels but was more flexible than the single strand stuff.

Many brands of made-up leaders were available in various finishes and hook sizes, including a wavy-wire "kelp cutter" for bass fishing. All serious fishermen learned to fashion with their fingers the "piano twist" followed by the crank turn that snapped off the tag end of wire tighter to the wraps than was possible with cutters. Only a few old-timers remember that trick.

The advantage of wire was its resistance to abrasion and its strength was useful for bouncing the catch in a time when fish under ten pounds were seldom gaffed. Drawbacks were its stiffness and weight that inhibited movement by small baits, and its tendency to become kinked at the hook end after a few catches.

Modern monofilament produces far more strikes than wire ever did, but also loses many more hooked fish. Wire leaders worked very well in a time of abundant fish stocks but are not really missed.

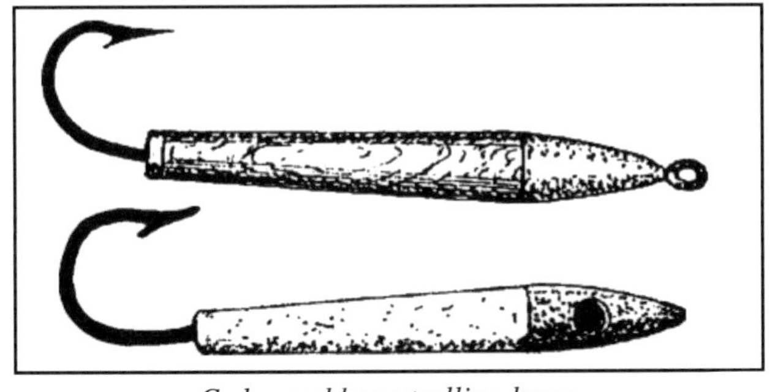

Cedar and bone trolling lures.

ARTIFICIAL BAITS

Before live bait fishing was introduced, trolling was the method for catching larger surface gamefish. Few of the artificial baits used were suited to cast-and-retrieve fishing. A West Coast favorite was the Al Wilson spoon, an elongated oval of stamped metal, slightly curved and cupped, with a single large hook dangling from the middle. C. F. Holder mentions it as a popular trolling lure as far back as 1910. Originally designed as a salmon bait, it had a violent wobbling action even at slow speeds.

Very similar was the chrome-plated Pflueger Record spoon, an Eastern entry which came along somewhat later. It was very effective when trolled for yellowtail and the large sizes were deadly for white seabass. At Catalina, trolling along the edge of the kelp east of Avalon with a six to eight inch spoon was long a productive method for taking seabass. It was easy to get their attention with the big flashy wobblers and I had good success with them as late as 1948.

Bendo! Long rods were standard in the old days.

The Knowles Automatic Striker spoon resembled the Wilson but had a slot in the center in which the hook eye was fixed while trolling. When a fish struck the hook would trip and slide to the end of the slot. The sudden stop was supposed to set the hook.

An early factory lure for albacore was the cedar jig. It was simply a cigar-sized cylinder of wood in its natural finish, weighted with a lead head and carrying a single large, black-enameled hook fixed through its centerline. The design was a very old one, probably derived from European sailing trollers who pursued "tunny" in the Bay of Biscay. Recently rediscovered by sportfishermen, cedars have proven exceedingly effective when trolled for tuna. The modern version has a centerline hole that allows the lure to ride up the leader in the manner of a feather bait.

Another jig from the same era is a factory made bone similar in appearance to the more common cedar jigs, but with some important differences. Instead of a hook eye at the nose, there is a hole in the lead head that connects to a recess that opens in the right side like an eye socket. A removable metal toggle pin would fit there around which a leader could be fastened and the pin reinserted in the recess, a most unusual arrangement. The jig is 5 3/4 inches in length and has a single black hook fixed in the cylindrical body.

There is a photo dated 1921 showing an angler posing with a sizeable bluefin tuna that was apparently taken with one of these odd lures. Hanging from a split bamboo rod, it is rigged to a wire leader with three box swivels and a torpedo sinker. The fisherman doesn't seem too happy, but he is wearing a rod socket that looks like a soup can. It couldn't have given him much protection to the groin.

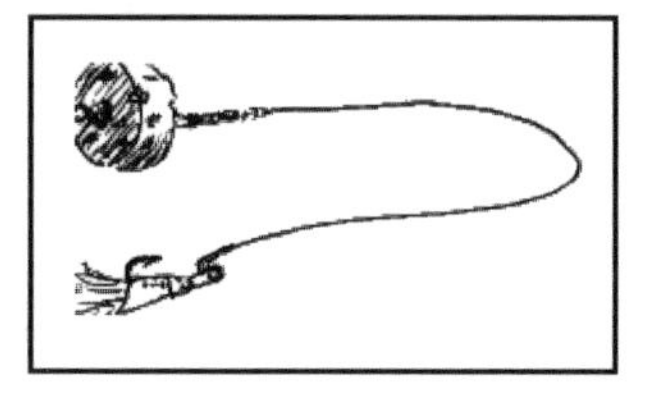

Cork and feather rig.

Immigrant Japanese fishermen introduced the feather and whalebone jigs that are still in use today. Lacking weight enough for easy casting, bones were never favored by party boat anglers. For commercial trolling they are true killers of all surface fish. My log shows a catch of 53 large yellowtail and 241 bonito over six pounds taken three miles outside Pt. Loma on Oct. 11, 1966—all on bone jigs in eight hours of fishing. Copied from successful bone jig designs, the famous plastic Baldys are frequently seen on albacore boat lines.

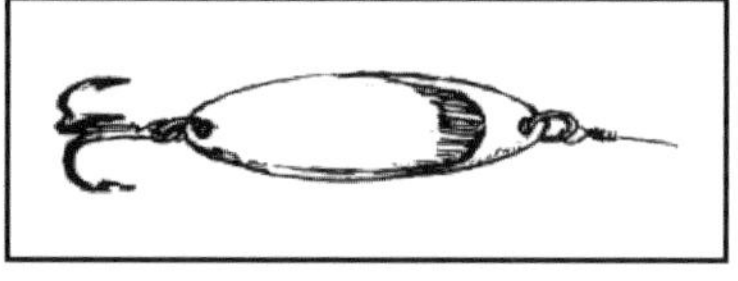

Dodger jig.

The Japanese trolling feathers are exactly the same as those of 60 or 70 years ago. Tin plated lead heads with glass eyes were standard. One model had pieces of iridescent abalone shell inlaid in the head.

For decent casting with linen lines, a lure weighing at least three ounces was required. It needed also to attract fish when cranked in with standard low gear-ratio reels. The need was filled by the Dodger, a bronze spoon plated with a satiny nickel finish. Slightly cupped on both sides, the Dodger was one of the few metal jigs with intrinsic wobble action. It was a deadly fish-catcher and the most popular lure available in the prewar years. The Streamline Dodger, a later model of chromed pot metal, sported a red stripe. "Iron" jigs now made for West Coast fishing are somewhat different in shape. Their design is derived mostly from old bone jig patterns.

Another extremely popular bait, the small Japanese fixed-hook feather jig, was by itself too light for easy casting. It was often trailed behind a sinker stuffed into the center hole of a net cork. The rig was seen most often on piers and barges. When retrieved, the splashing cork got the attention of any bonito in the area. Casting for barracuda required a sinker attached ahead of the leader. So deadly was it that the awkwardness of the arrangement was overlooked. Today the feather is available with an enlarged head to aid casting. The lure is still a good one for bonito.

Hetzel jigs appeared as early as 1935. One model was apparently an early attempt at reproducing in plastic the traditional Japanese bone jigs. It probably was tried during World War II when bones were unobtainable. The lure was a light yellowish color with a red patch at the tail of its typically boat-shaped body. It had a metal reinforcing plate set in the nose to take the strain of the wobble ring, and the name "HETZEL" was stamped on the flat top. The method of securing the hook was unique. Instead of a screw or rivet the hook on the Hetzel had an extra-long eyeless shank that turned downward in a short 90 degree angle to fit snugly into a hole drilled through the jig. The heavy wire fastening the after end was soldered to the hook shank, another innovation. The whole rig was very strong but it would not have been as easy to replace a hook as it was on the Japanese bones. Perhaps screws and rivets were hard-to-get wartime items when the jig was in production.

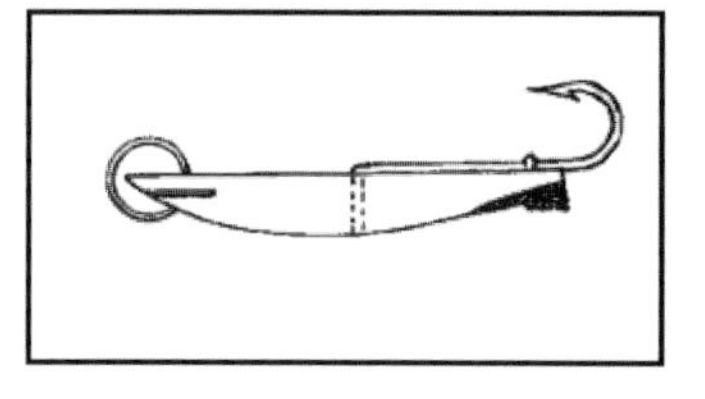

Hetzel jig.

In the years immediately following WW II some new gadgets appeared. Still to be found is the Spoofer, but the Clyde's Clobber and the Vivif rubber "toad" are becoming somewhat rare. Interesting items were the metal Hoedra "Sara Deen" and the "Hoodwink."

The Bendo Jig was 6¾ inches of a sort of pliable plastic with a malleable metal spine. It was made by Fish-Eze Products of Los Angeles and the idea was to bend the thing until it wobbled or spun according to the whim of the user. It had a sort of dark cream color with three reddish bands in it. There were five little chevron shapes molded onto the flat top surface, apparently for decoration. The bottom had a rather deep hump, but the bait was too light for its bulk.

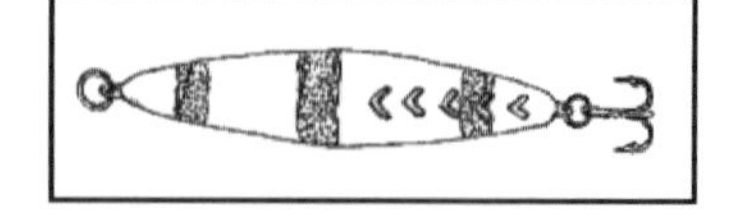

Bendo jig.

Presumably all these lures were field tested but never caught on with the public. Some disappeared for reasons unknown. I made good catches of barracuda and yellowtail with the Spoofer and Clobber when I used them in the 1950s.

In the early days of sportfishing, Eastern tackle factories turned out a multitude of wood and metal baits. Many were beefed up versions of freshwater bass plugs, not really effective in the Pacific. Most were short lived as they did not hook fish consistently, were too expensive or were awkward to use. A few worked well enough but were supplanted by improved designs that fished even better.

No Eastern-designed lures that I can think of have had outstanding success in our area although a few became temporarily popular. Our West Coast jigs work very well in any of the world's oceans.

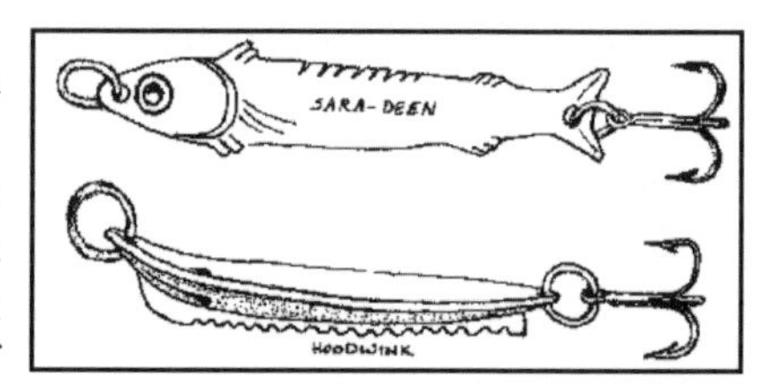

Sara Deen and Hoodwink.

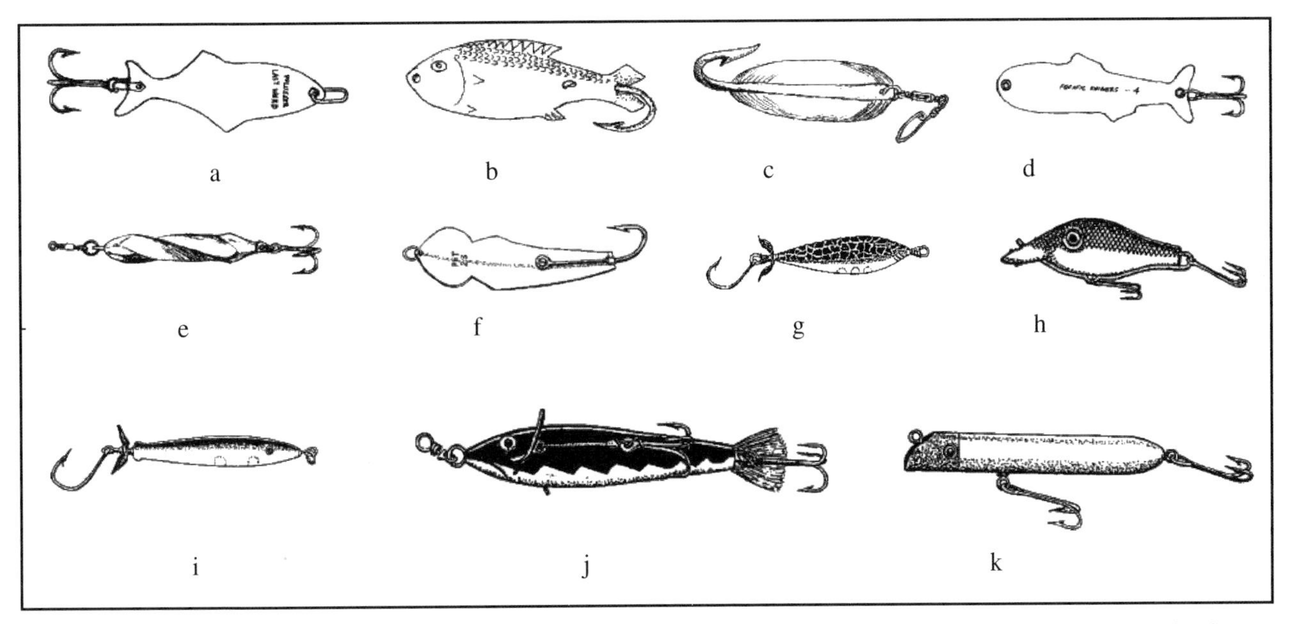

Lures of metal and wood were tried without notable success. a: Pflueger "Last Word." b & c: Metal spoons of unknown brands. d: Pacific Shiners. e: Spinner jig. f: Pflueger "Pet" spoon. g: Heddon "Coast Minnow." h: P & K "Lippy." i: Pflueger "Bearcat." j: British wooden Herring. k: South Bend "Tarporeno."

In the 30s, long bamboo rods were preferred for all-around fishing.

Tackle extremes: Gent in background uses a three-six rig (six ounce rod, six feet long, six-thread line,) then considered ultra-light. Old-timer in foreground prefers a handline.

Scotty Lacade's OWL II in her commercial configuration. Note jackpole and handline anglers fishing over canvas covered bait net and black seabass being boated amidship. The majority of early sport boats were converted from similar craft.

In this 1927 photo Scotty Lacade's KITTY A. awaits her turn to load at Santa Monica pier. PALISADES is alongside.

Chapter 3
TO SEA IN A TUB

PLUNGING ON THE "PALI"

In 1932 I made my first trips on a "live bait boat," as party fishing craft were called. Compared to the yacht-like craft of today, the vessel was incredibly primitive. She was the PALISADES, owned by the Morris Pleasure Fishing Company of Santa Monica. The boat was typical of general purpose commercial hulls known as albacore chasers. Built during the 'teens and 'twenties, they supplied the South Coast's booming canneries with tuna, mackerel and sardines.

The hull was about 55 feet long, round bottomed, narrow in beam, with a straight stem and a horseshoe stern. She was painted white with black trim and the bait tank and inboard side of the bulwarks were painted red. To ease the handling of nets the afterdeck was close to the water. Above the deck was a low bulwark about 18 inches high with one-inch open scuppers all around. To meet insurance requirements for passenger service, a chain lifeline stretched through T's atop pipe stanchions inserted in the bulwark rail.

W. K., sister to PALISADES.

Running from bow to stern on the inboard side of the bulwarks was a narrow wooden bench. At 18 inch intervals a stripe was painted on the bench to mark the seating space allotted each angler. The authorized load was 53 souls, if memory serves. No galley or shelter of any kind was provided for the passengers.

Amidships was a small pilot house with a low cabin trunk leading forward. Under the trunk sat a huge Standard gasoline engine about three feet high with magneto spark and little petcocks on each cylinder head to receive drops of priming fuel. This mechanical monstrosity was started by inserting an iron bar in holes around the rim of the massive flywheel and cranking vigorously until ignition took place in one or more of the four cylinders. It required a good deal of strength and stamina on the part of the cranker and fast action closing the petcocks, some of which were open to release compression. When started, the mill

FAITH, Morris half-day boat.

exhausted through an upright dry stack with a loud, deep-toned "buggeda, buggeda, buggeda" sound that rings clearly in my ears to this day.

Forward of the engine on either side were a pair of dingy bunks containing oil cans, tools and assorted junk. A small "head" about the size of a phone booth was mounted atop the central hatch. A large box for storing the cork lifejackets bridged the space between the roofs of the head and pilot house. Alongside the house was a hand-operated bilge pump. In the bow were wooden bitts, a coil of heavy manila rope and the old-fashioned anchor which was raised by "Norwegian steam," (i.e. by hand, without mechanical aids).

On the afterdeck was the wooden bait tank whose pump was driven by the main engine or a small gas auxiliary. Circulating water poured like rain through holes drilled in the top of the tank, a much less efficient arrangement than used today. The overflow pipe and chute were above deck and emptied overside. The space between the sides of the tank and the seating bench was very narrow, less than two feet.

The fare on the PALI, as she was known, for an all-day, 8 a.m. to 4 p.m. trip was two dollars. When the boat was lightly loaded, I was able to wheedle my way aboard for half fare. A boarding line was formed by order of ticket purchase and the early birds got the stern. There was no rotation; latecomers, deadheads and half-fares made do in the bow. I learned not to mind this too much. A lot of drifting for halibut was done and the bow was a better location for that fishing than the stern.

Boarding was via steep gangway steps always slippery with salt and slime. Once aboard the anglers chose the available seats, stowed their tackle boxes and sacks beneath the bench, and sat shoulder to shoulder while chugging to the first hot spot. If bait was not aboard, considerable time sometimes passed waiting for a successful haul by the bait boat.

"Plunger" was the somewhat derisive term used by crewmen for an inept fishing novice. It was amazing how many men came fishing dressed in their vested business suits, complete with collar, tie and felt hat, as if they were going to an office. Some of the "plungers" not only fished like farmers but also looked the part in bib overalls of several types including trainman's stripes and carpenter's whites. Items of olive drab army uniform from the Great War were also much favored. The old corduroy pants I wore, stiff with salt, slime and fish blood, were my poor Mother's washday despair.

Tackle in use ranged from handlines wound on a stick to cane jackpoles, and all sorts of rod and reel combinations. I never saw a barracuda gaffed on the PALI. All were bounced, including logs. In fact, the only fish I ever saw gaffed were largish halibut, seabass and yellowtail. Anglers unhooked and sacked their own fish.

Handling numbers of lively fish was hard on the fingers. Sore hands and fish poisoning infections were common. Sacks and stringers were kept on deck or hanging over the side from a stanchion. When fishing was good one could hardly walk about the deck without treading on a bulging gunny bag.

If the sea was at all choppy, water gushed through the open scuppers keeping fish and feet well cooled. A ride "uphill" against the slop on a windy day left every person on deck drenched by flying spray and green water sloshing over the low weather bulwark. In a beam sea the narrow, round-bottomed hull of the PALI rolled violently. When too many soaked souls fled to the lee side the skipper, to maintain stability, would order some back to the weather side. Salty young teenagers like myself would test our sea legs by standing unsupported while keeping watch for victims of seasickness. We were only too happy to dispose of any leftovers in their lunch bags.

Each passenger lugged his own fish off the boat.

On arrival at the pier each passenger lugged his own tackle and fish up the landing steps and soaked, filthy, tired and contented we squished off in wet shoes to our separate ways.

In 1936 the boat was modernized somewhat with a diesel engine and other improvements, but the first strong impressions she made on me are the ones I remember best.

This reminiscence would not be complete without a tribute to Captain Orrin Winfield, longtime skipper of the old PALISADES, a rugged, kindly, patient man from whom I learned much more than simply how to fish.

This 1935 photo of VALENCIA is one of my favorites. The scene is typical for partyboats in the 'twenties and 'thirties. The boat operated from Newport Pier. Mast and boom are relics of commercial days when they were used for spotting fish and brailing the catch. When the boat was less crowded the jackpoles by the mast would be used by

Togetherness on the VALENCIA

the crew to supplement income. The plungers, squeezed together elbow to elbow, have several hookups going on their long Calcutta sticks. The gent in overalls will be hollering, "Low bridge" as he prepares to cast. Bulging sacks hang from the chain lifeline. The photo was taken from the bow of a neighboring boat. Such togetherness was common, especially when fishing a barracuda school, to share chum and ward off circling jig boats.

THE SAN DIEGO STYLE

The photos show the type of vessels developed at SanDiego in the early days. They are part of the fleet sailing from the foot of Broadway and adjacent landings in the downtown area. Only sight-seeing excursions now leave from that location.

The majority were converted commercial boats with single screw propulsion providing little in the way of comfort for passengers. The latter sat in the open on drop-leaf benches fastened along the bulwarks. The wobbly pipe-and-chain lifelines used on the first sport boats were replaced with a solid wooden railing. Developed in San Diego as a safety measure, the wooden rail provided bracing for anglers battling heavy fish. It also served as a support for the heavy sacks of fish that were hung on the iron hooks spaced along the underside of the rail. So practical was this arrangement that it soon spread up the coast and is still in use today.

Oakley Hall's VIRGINIA.

Oakley Hall's VIRGINIA, Guy Tadlock's YELLOWTAIL and Frank Kiessig's SPORTFISHER were somewhat above the average size of boats used at the northern landings. Larger hulls had room for deckhouses containing sizeable galleys and some shelter for passengers. Shelves on the after side of the house provided the gear and tackle storage eliminated by the drop-leaf seats, a feature still in use. The cleaned and repainted fish holds afforded sleeping space to those willing to lie on bare planks. A few bunks in the former crew's quarters were also available for the more fastidious. Competition resulted in the generally high standards of maintenance and operation that were a feature of the San Diego Style.

SEA ANGLER, the first large built-for-the-purpose sportfishing boat, was launched for the Star & Crescent Boat Co. in January 1934. Built at the cost of $20,000 (big bucks in the 'thirties) her twin 80 hp diesels were supposed to give her a speed of 13 knots, very swift for a displacement hull. On her first test run she made it from the Coronado Islands to the Broadway Pier in two hours and 15 minutes. Fast and

SEA ANGLER

comfortable, she made all her competitors in the sport fleet obsolete. So popular was she that two years later a newer, faster vessel, the STAR ANGLER, was built and until recently she was still in service at a northern landing.

To meet the competition Frank Kiessig built SPORTFISHER II, the second angling partyboat ever to be built specifically for that purpose. She was a 65-footer licensed to carry 75 passengers and could sleep 18 in comfortable bunks with crisp sheets and pillowcases. It was this boat with her 2,000 mile range that pioneered long range fishing trips to Mexican waters.

Then as now, many San Diego fishermen were from out of town. To help preserve the fish until anglers could get their catches home, deckhands provided a cleaning service. The fish were merely gutted and the heads left on, but it was considerable extra work when the catch was large. A few tips were earned, but no fee was asked or expected. For a long time the southern fleet was unique in offering this free service, another mark of the standard-setting San Diego Style.

Backing into the slip, 1937.

H&M Landing has to be one of the longevity champs in the sportfishing fleet. The business took form when four San Diego water taxi operators, Bill and Tony Hoss, Howard Minor and Ralph Miller, bought the MASCOT 2, once owned by veteran skipper Mel Shears, and sent her out from the foot of Broadway. On her first trip, April 6, 1935, she returned with 135 yellowtail for 35 passengers, an auspicious start.

Howard Minor, one of the original founders of H&M, was associated with the landing from 1935 to 1968. His interest in sportfishing began in 1934 with trips on Oakley Hall's NEW POINT LOMA barge and the boat SEA ANGLER. He and Mrs. Minor caught 10 yellowtail from the barge, out of a total of 76 landed on July 4.

Turned on by fishing, Minor rigged his water taxi NAVA with a homemade bait tank and powered the pump with a washing machine motor. The arrangement worked well enough on the frequent trips he made that summer. On September 15, Minor and partner Ralph "Barney" Miller took the latter's taxi BARNEY GOOGLE III out for their first try at marlin fishing. Each landed a spikebill, baited with trolled flying fish. No wonder they became enthused enough to go into the fishing business the following spring!

There was plenty of competition from Kiessig, Schipper and others, so the water taxis were retained for several years with some being converted for charter fishing. Old-timers will perhaps remember those unique craft, the WORRIERS and the BARNEY GOOGLES. San Diego and San Pedro were home ports for the Navy's Pacific Fleet and most of the ships moored out in the bays. Sailors coming and going on liberty or business provided continuous employment for a 24-hour taxi service.

Underway for an afternoon trip.

In 1937 the MASCOT III was purchased and converted for sportfishing. Originally a sailing vessel, she was launched in 1888 and used in the coastal trade, hauling live turtles and onyx from Mexico. Already 51 years from launch when acquired by H&M, she probably holds the record as longest-lived sport boat, being 69 years of age when finally disposed of in 1957. Her massive construction no doubt contributed to her longevity.

Despite her heaviness and slow speed, MASCOT III was popular with anglers and I frequently fished from her myself. She often ran two trips daily, departing at 2 a.m. for the Coronados and at 2 p.m. for the Point Loma kelp beds. The fare to the islands was $3 and to the kelp it was $2.

Business continued to thrive until World War II came along. Less strategically located landings, such as those at Newport Beach and Santa Monica, were able to remain in operation during the hostilities, but the San Diego fleet was forced to close down for the duration.

Fishing runs were resumed in the spring of 1946 and in 1949 the landing moved to its present Point Loma location. New boats were added from time to time including the NEW MASCOT in 1957, MALIHINI in 1960, H&M 85 in 1965 and the aluminum catamaran SPEED TWIN in 1971. Today the landing is home port for a fleet of over 20 modern sportfishers. Ownership has changed but the business carries on in the traditional fashion.

Water taxi type charter boat.

AMECO

Fatal accidents in the sportboat fleet have been remarkably few considering the countless operating hours. The present strict regulations governing passenger boat construction, equipment and operation were all enacted as a result of rare mishaps occurring in the past.

One of the worst disasters to befall a fishing party boat occurred on Memorial Day, 1930, when the AMECO capsized off Topanga Canyon with the loss of nineteen lives. For days blaring headlines filled the local newspapers as official inquiries attempted to fix blame for the tragedy. Because of vagueness and omissions in the laws, no liability was ever determined.

AMECO and PALISADES

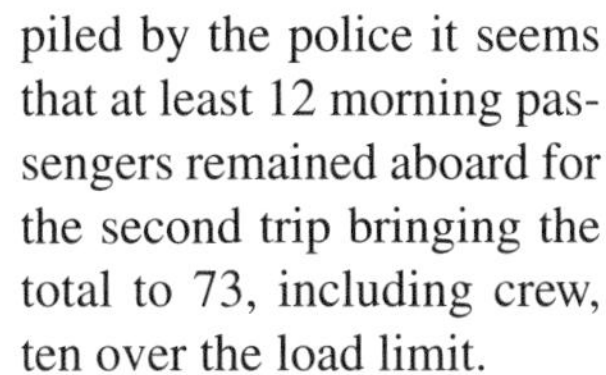

To understand such a happening we need to be aware of the conditions under which boats operated at the time. We also need to be assured that a similar accident is extremely unlikely today.

Identical in hull design and deck arrangement to her sister vessel PALISADES, the 54-foot AMECO was typical of sport boats engaged in local fishing before World War II. She was a converted commercial craft of 14 gross tons with narrow beam, horseshoe stern, round bottom and low freeboard aft.

State law allowed boats of this type to carry up to 63 passengers. The U.S. Steamboat Inspection Service issued licenses and could penalize operators for negligence but had no jurisdiction over vessels less than 15 tons. It was pretty much left to insurance companies to decide whether small passenger boats were adequately equipped for safety.

AMECO was owned by the company founded by the pioneering Capt. T. J. Morris at Santa Monica. Morris himself had drowned four years earlier while attempting to salvage his boat W. K.

On May 30 AMECO was running half day trips. The weather was less than ideal but increasing winds and rough seas did not discourage the 59 happy holiday anglers who bought tickets for the afternoon trip. From later lists compiled by the police it seems that at least 12 morning passengers remained aboard for the second trip bringing the total to 73, including crew, ten over the load limit.

After several hours fishing at the Bubble Hole spot the anchor was pulled about 4:15. Seas were running high by this time and considerable water splashed aboard as the boat turned toward the pier. The AMECO was running in the trough when a wave slapped the starboard bow drenching passengers on that side with spray. Many of the wetted ones rushed to the opposite rail. At that moment, as she still listed to port, a huge swell loomed over the launch. In an instant AMECO rolled bottom up, flinging all her people into the sea. In the indescribable confusion and horror of the moment some sank at once. Others more fortunate clawed at the upturned keel or clung to lifejackets and flotsam spilled from the wreck.

Luckily another fishing boat, Dick Hernage's FREEDOM, was nearby and was able to commence rescue operations within minutes. Those floundering in the water were picked up first and some 35 to 40 survivors were hauled aboard. As she too became overloaded, many feared for the stability of the FREEDOM herself, but veteran skipper Joe Fudge returned the shaken crowd safely to the pier. Other craft including the PALISADES, sister to the AMECO, raced to the site. In all, 54 souls were rescued and 19 declared dead or missing. If the FREEDOM had not been close at hand the loss of life would undoubtedly have been much greater.

A larger number of deaths occurred on Sept. 24, 1939 when the SPRAY, fishing near Point Mugu, capsized in a

Three lives of the MUSIC: Before live bait, with bait net in 1930, and in the early postwar years.

sudden 70-mile-per hour gale. Twenty four people drowned including skipper Earl Steckel and his wife. Only two survivors managed to swim ashore. News reports of the storm had a total of 45 persons lost at sea along the South Coast. Due probably to the overall losses, the SPRAY disaster got much less press coverage than the AMECO.

Second only to the AMECO tragedy in fatalities was the loss of the charter boat SPARE TIME in July 1952, also in Santa Monica Bay. A butane explosion demolished the vessel about 14 miles offshore when returning from an albacore trip. Out of twelve passengers aboard only three survived.

KIAORA was originally a yacht.

KIAORA modernized.

Kiessig's SPORTFISHER at her downtown berth. Her success led to the development of long range fishing.

Billy Rice's popular SUNSHINE II fished at Catalina.

Deckhand guts tuna on a San Diego boat, SAN ANTONIO, c. 1932. There was no charge for this service. Waist level cleaning boards did not come into use until the late 'fifties. Watching angler trolls. There were no bunks.

Avalon charter launch. Big game fishing began in boats like these.

LIGHT was a basic albacore chaser converted for sportfishing, c. 1925.

TOURIST took parties before a live bait system was available.

OWL acting as tender to the barge OLYMPIC. Note jackpoles and absence of liferails. 1926.

Party boat fishing at its crudest. JOHNSON NO. 1 off Santa Cruz.

The author worked as a deckhand aboard rebuilt VALENCIA in 1940.

A sampling of sportfishing boats from the Golden Years is shown above. The abundance of fish close to piers and ports made their employment practicable and profitable. Compare them with today's fast, comfortable, well-equipped vessels.

The steel bark STAR OF SCOTLAND as a fishing barge, c. 1930.

PAPROCA was the first barge, and very successful too.

Chapter 4
THE BARGE STORY

Imagine if you will a lofty sailing ship that once tramped the oceans of the world, serving as a platform for hundreds of anglers pursuing the pleasures of saltwater sportfishing. The big steel four-masted bark STAR OF SCOTLAND with rigging intact and yards still crossed on her towering masts, was a familiar sight off Santa Monica from 1930-37. A veteran of stormy Cape Horn passages, she was one of some 37 old windjammers pressed into service as fishing barges in the years from 1925 to 1940.

The price of a day's fishing varied between ports but was competitive and ranged from as little as $1 to as much as $3. Bait and bamboo jackpoles were free. Night fishing under lights was usually available in the summer and parties, dancing and gambling were additional activities aboard some of the hulks.

Generally, the barges were stable and rode easily on the swells, providing room to move about or lounge comfortably while fishing or merely relaxing. A galley was open for warm food and cold drinks and it was a time of ten-cent hamburgers, two-bit chili and bottled pop for a nickel.

Eliminated were the drawbacks of seasickness, wet feet and drenching spray so often encountered on the mobile "live bait boats." Barges were seldom anchored more than two miles offshore and were serviced throughout the day by launches making regular round trips from the home piers. It was the ideal venue for a family outing.

Mackerel were the most numerous catch from barges, but many bonito, barracuda and halibut were also taken. Extra excitement was generated when schools of yellowtail or white seabass showed up and large catches of these species were sometimes made, particularly from the San Diego hulks.

Most of the former sailing ships had a "jewfish bridge," a special platform built on the bowsprit, which was reserved for the dedicated black seabass angler. There he could mount his heavy tackle well clear of the other fishermen while soaking a bait. The giant bass were plentiful in those days and a great many were taken from barges. Transferring to the shoreboat was often necessary if a hooked bass was a monster that needed chasing down before it could be brought to gaff.

According to the Dept. of Fish & Game, the first fishing barge was the PAPROCA, owned by A. B. Hohenshell of Long Beach. Opening for business in 1921, she was a resounding success, serving over 100,000 eager anglers in the first five years of operation. PAPROCA was a simple rectangular scow hull with few amenities, but was popular nonetheless. There is also some photo evidence that more than one scow barge operated off Long Beach at the time.

Hans Carstensen placed the first barge at Redondo in the spring of 1922, and added two more the following year. The barge concept underwent a sudden expansion in 1925 when a number of ex-sailing ships were put into service. By the next year there were no less than 21 vessels doing business along the South Coast. Apart from a couple in Monterey Bay, this motley fleet was concentrated off southern California from Santa Barbara to San Diego. The barges were immensely popular in the years before the Second World War as desirable fish were abundant and the cost of fishing was minimal

The idea of using obsolete sailing ships as barges seems to have occurred to several entrepreneurs simultaneously. Many fine old windships, driven from the high seas by more efficient steamers, were laid up in backwaters and available for very little money. A number were procured by moving picture producers for such film epics as "Moby Dick," "Old Ironsides," "Mutiny on the Bounty" and others. Some of these later became fishing barges, generally being altered to reduce rolling by removal of their masts. With few exceptions the ships were wooden schooners and barkentines built on the West Coast as lumber carriers. The hulks were usually large enough to accommodate upwards of 200 fishermen at a time.

Webb Monstad purchased the barkentine LAHAINA for $600 in January, 1925. By August she was in barge service at Redondo, as was the barkentine FULLERTON for the same owner. In March of 1925 Capt. Olaf Olsen brought the whaling bark NARWHAL and the schooner CHARLES BROWN to Santa Monica. Under tow for barge duty, Rube Shafer's schooner MURIEL was wrecked in the Newport channel on July 3, 1925. The steel bark GRATIA was bought by William Storey in August, 1925 and Hans Carstensen and A. R. Paulesen purchased the schooner WILLIAM BOWDEN in the same year. These were among the first, but by no means the last, of the ex-windjammer barges.

Steel bark GRATIA rigged down for barge service. Note long jewfish platform on bowsprit.

With the exception of Olsen's ships at Santa Monica and the MURIEL at Newport, all the early ship barges first began work off Redondo and it would appear that Hans Carstensen was the prime mover. Altogether there were at least 37 ex-sailing ships in service as barges between 1925

Schooner SAMAR at Catalina. The sign on her side advertises "Fishing, Dining, Dancing, Cabins."

and 1942. Some also doubled as gambling casinos or were used as way stations between shore and gaming craft.

Three metal-hulled sailing ships served as barges: GRATIA, OLYMPIC II and STAR OF SCOTLAND. The latter was a large ship that rode so high when empty of cargo that side galleries were constructed to put fishermen closer to the water. Of the wooden barges, only SAMAR carried similar galleries and KOHALA had sponsons around her stern section. On the rest fishing was done from the deck, but in some cases high bulwarks were cut down to waist level. SAMAR and GLENDALE began fishing with masts still erect, but they were later removed. Only STAR OF SCOTLAND retained her masts at full length for the duration of her fishing career.

When several barges were located in one area such as Santa Monica Bay, the competition for business sometimes became fierce. Price cutting brought on well-publicized threats and counter threats among the owners. In the Depression year of 1931 the price of a day's fishing at Redondo reached a new low when William Storey, owner of the GRATIA, reduced his fare from the standard $1 to 50 cents. Webb Monstad followed suit as did barge owners at Long Beach, Manhattan and Ocean Park. Charles Arnold, skipper of STAR OF SCOTLAND, stuck to the old price and declared that if he could not operate for the profit that only a dollar fee allowed, he would advertise free fishing and run his launches gratis.

There was a good deal of barge movement along the South Coast as owners sought a profitable operating area. Some were bought and sold several times during their careers. Two examples come to mind: GEORGE E. BILLINGS, a fine five-masted schooner, was bought by the South Coast Land Co. in 1926 for use as a fishing barge, museum and restaurant for the guests of the Hotel Del Mar. The scheme failed and the ship was sold to Robert Oefinger in 1930. He brought her to Ocean Park where she remained a popular attraction for the next eleven years. The barkentine KOHALA, after duty off Hermosa, was towed to San Diego in 1932 by her new owners, Chris Enholm and Woody Shortt. Unable to overcome competition from the two barges already established off Point Loma, KOHALA was again sold north and wound up at Redondo.

To avoid the winter gales some barges were towed to sheltered waters in San Pedro, Wilmington or Long Beach and laid up from fall to spring. Others remained at anchor all winter and many became storm casualties, parting their anchor chains and drifting ashore.

Once beached the old wooden hulls proved to be unsalvageable and in most cases were burnt where they

FULLERTON ashore at Redondo, 1926.

THOMAS P. EMIGH beached in April, 1932. Three other barges were also wrecked by the same storm.

lay. Only three were hauled off. The GEORGINA, once a graceful four-masted barkentine, was refloated after grounding at Hermosa Beach in 1935, but was so leaky that she was scrapped shortly thereafter. The IRENE sank in January of 1937 from leaks caused by her stranding two months earlier. The GEORGE U. HIND broke away from her tow and stranded at Solana Beach in April of 1936. After salvage by the Coast Guard she was relocated at Oceanside. Two months later she was again beached in a sinking condition. A December storm finished her off.

The Redondo area was a regular graveyard for barges. WILLIAM BOWDEN was the first wreck on February 12, 1926, and the FULLERTON followed in May of 1927. The storm of April 20, 1932 claimed four more off the Southern California Coast: GRATIA, THOMAS P. EMIGH, CHARLES BROWN and the ex-ferry MELROSE. The LAHAINA was wrecked in 1933, OCEANIA VANCE in 1936 and the IRENE sank in 1937. Fortunately, no lives were lost in these multiple disasters.

Other strandings took place up and down the coast: ESTHER BUHNE at Newport in 1927, MINNIE A. CAINE at Santa Monica in 1939, and ANNIE M. ROLPH at Rocky Point in 1942. Most of the other ex-sailers died of old age and neglect at Terminal Island or in Cerritos Channel. A number were burned for scrap or disposed as a liability.

Two of the old windjammers were run down by steamers. The JANE L. STANFORD was rammed by the coastal liner HUMBOLDT off Santa Barbara in 1929 and the remains were later blown up at Santa Rosa Island. The OLYMPIC II was sunk by the Japanese steamer SAKITO MARU off San Pedro.

Although the former sailing ships were the most interesting and romantic, another 60 or so vessels of various types such as scows, ferries, landing craft, tugs, kelp harvesters, steamers and a former World War One Q-boat were also employed as non-mobile sportfishers. Notable was the SIERRA, ex-VIRGINIA OLSON, a wooden-hulled steam lumber schooner of a type once numerous on the Pacific Coast. She enjoyed a long career as a barge off White's Point until her owner, Capt. Heigoro Endo, was interned when the war began. Sadly, the ship simply rotted away in Cerritos Channel.

KOHALA at Redondo.

KOHALA (or Hawaiian flower) met the strangest fate of any fishing barge. Once a beautiful four-masted barkentine with a glistening white hull, she sailed the seas for over twenty years before being sold for a barge in 1927. After service at Hermosa Beach and San Diego, she wound up at Redondo with Daisy Monstad as her owner. There she remained, now sporting a green hull with orange trim. In spite of her rather garish paint job, she was a popular attraction for hundreds of anglers.

The terrible shock of the attack on Pearl Harbor had a profound effect on the West Coast. Pleasure boating activity ceased and KOHALA was a lonely hulk manned only by her master and a young watchman, Jack Kitchen.

KOHALA under sail.

On Christmas Eve of 1941 I happened to be serving in the minesweeper U.S.S. COURSER which was sweeping the approaches to San Pedro Harbor. As I watched a nearby steamer, a violent explosion tossed lumber from her deckload high in the air. S.S. ABSAROKA had just been blasted by a torpedo from the Japanese submarine I-19. My little ship was unable to take offensive action as we had no sonar and our main battery consisted of two .30 caliber machine guns. As naval strength was concentrated elsewhere, alarm and consternation spread among shoreside officials.

That dark night Kitchen believed he heard a strange noise resembling the hum of a diesel engine. Unable to communicate with the pier, it was Christmas Day before Kitchen got ashore and was able to notify the Coast Guard. The Army was informed and jittery generals became convinced that an enemy lurked near Redondo. Two artillery pieces were set up on the Horseshoe Pier and .50 caliber machine guns were emplaced along the shore. Planes from March Field appeared overhead and bombs rained down. Trigger-happy soldiers began shooting from shore and pandemonium prevailed. When the smoke cleared, only pieces of the barge, fortunately unmanned, remained. Later a navy plane wasted a depth bomb on some of the floating wreckage. Next day headlines in the Los Angeles

Times screamed: "Army Flyer Sinks Coast Raider. Air Filled With Debris as Nippon Submarine is Destroyed." Alas, the debris was only the remains of poor KOHALA, innocent victim of wartime hysteria and "friendly fire." The sub was long gone and escaped to fight on for two more years before being sunk near the Marshall Islands.

Barge fishing, c. 1926.

The barge owners were a mixture of practical seamen and shoreside businessmen. Several were retired sailing ship masters, perhaps motivated to find one last use for the windships they loved.

Capt. Olaf C. Olsen was probably the most colorful of the owners. A native of Norway, he went to sea in sail before 1900 and eventually wound up in Santa Monica. He began a barge operation with the whaling bark NARWHAL and the little schooner CHARLES BROWN. He later acquired the FOX and the MINNIE A. CAINE.

Olsen was very popular and well-known in the decade before the war and his enthusiastic boosting of bay fishing earned him the title of "Santa Monica Olsen." Always ready with a story pitched in a heavy Norwegian accent, he was the epitome of the salty deep-sea sailor and certainly looked the part. He was stocky but powerful in build and always wore a seaman's billed cap and smoked a pipe. One of his friends and customers was the cartoonist Segar who created the character "Popeye," using Olsen as the prototype. A

Olsen's FOX at Santa Monica, 1938.

shoreboat deckhand also caught Segar's eye and became the model for the hamburger-addicted Wimpy.

In 1924 San Diego businessman and ardent angler Frank Kiessig purchased a surplus navy coal barge and readied her for fishing. Heavily timbered and copper sheathed against marine borers, the barge was 144 feet long with a 40-foot beam. To make fish handling and gaffing easier, a fishing gallery was constructed around the sides to be only four feet above the water. A ten-room cabin was constructed on deck with two bunks in each room fitted with clean sheets and blankets. The deckhouse included a galley, tackle shop and office. There was a bait tank with eight hand wells and two reserve bait receivers were secured under the stern platform.

Christened IKE WALTON, Kiessig's barge opened for business April 1926. She was moored at the La Jolla kelp beds and anglers were ferried to the waiting shore boat in a skiff rowed through the mild surf of the Cove. Dean Hueck, the skiffmaster, claimed an unblemished record of never getting a passenger wet! The barge fare was $2 with live bait guaranteed. Excellent fishing assured success and there were many overnight customers.

Kiessig allowed no handline fishing and would whip out a knife and cut those he discovered. Smiling, he would remind the offending fisherman of barge policy and loan him a rent rod at no charge "one time only."

Increasing logistic problems associated with the La Jolla location were eased by moving the IKE WALTON to Point Loma for the 1929 season. In 1932 Kiessig sold the WALTON and turned his attention to the booming partyboat fishery at the Coronado Islands. He went on to pioneer the first long range trips with specially built boats.

A former kelp harvesting vessel was pressed into barge service by Oakley Hall, owner of San Diego's Star & Crescent fleet of tugs, water taxis and ferries, on April 30, 1928. Named POINT LOMA, the barge was moored at the Drop Off, an area near the kelp beds that provides prime sport to this day. The fishing was at times, fabulous, as catches of yellowtail and white seabass were commonplace on the old hulk. For example: Over 200 yellowtail from 10 to 25 pounds landed September 8, 1930; a

IKE WALTON off La Jolla, 1926.

NEW POINT LOMA.

nine yellowtail per rod average catch on June 9, 1931; twenty-five white seabass to 28 pounds taken August 15, 1930, and 250-pound black seabass boated on August 3, 1930. Fishing for lesser species such as barracuda, bass and bonito was generally excellent.

Inspired by the success of his barge operation, Hall in 1932 bought the three-masted schooner GLENDALE to replace the aged PT. LOMA. Extensive alterations were made on the windjammer at Hall's shipyard. The after bulwarks were cut down to deck level and a wide fishing platform was built over the stern. Two big deck houses were erected enclosing bunks for 30, a galley and a ladies' lounge. Promenade decks with picnic tables and awnings topped the houses. A "Bachelors' Hall" was located in the fo'c'sle for those who wished to read or play cards. Bait wells holding 40 tons of water and 100,000 sardines were put into the hull. When completed she was advertised as a "fishing palace" and the "world's finest barge."

Opening for business in May 1932 the NEW POINT LOMA, ex-GLENDALE, quickly rang up impressive catches. On May 19, 30 passengers sacked 170 yellowtail and 10 white seabass. Such scores led the bargemaster to lament that the fishermen became spoiled and were disappointed if they didn't catch yellowtail. There was plenty of good fishing for other species. A great run of barracuda occurred in 1933 and one angler bounced 42 "snakes" in less than three hours casting a cork and trailing feather jig, a rig usually used to catch bonito from piers.

The only marlin ever caught from a stationary barge was taken on the NEW POINT LOMA on August 9, 1935. Malcolm Huey of Calexico hooked the spike on a sardine fly-lined for yellowtail. It took 50 minutes to land on 12-thread (36 pound) line, wire leader and 3/0 hook. Three gaffs and a couple shots from the skipper's rifle were needed to subdue the marlin before it could be lifted aboard. It weighed in at 200 pounds. Hooking billfish from anchored sportboats at the Coronado Islands was not uncommon in those days. That same year I saw three hookups at once from boats on the weather side of North Island.

Fishing on the barges to the north was seldom as productive, but they had their good times and remained popular. Many were profitable and well-maintained. One such was the five-masted schooner GEORGE E. BILLINGS, moored for ten seasons off Ocean Park.

In the summer of 1936 I was employed for two months as deckhand on MARDI GRAS, the shoreboat serving the BILLINGS. When approaching the pier my task was to balance on the slippery foredeck of the launch and plop the eye of a heavy manila springline over a huge iron hook hanging from the pilings. After hooking on, the engine was gunned and the rudder put hard aport to lay the boat against the pilings as passengers boarded or debarked. In rough weather or at low tide it became somewhat risky but it was the method for loading boats at all piers along the coast.

When not handling the springline I was kept busy polishing brass, swabbing the deck, and wiping moisture from the seats. When the sea was choppy, an important chore was to rub a plug of chewing tobacco on the pilot's window. The oil from the plug would shed the salt spray that otherwise impeded the skipper's vision. That I often got thoroughly soaked while performing this service mattered not at all.

The first of two shifts began at 0500 when the two-man crew lowered a skiff from the pierhead derrick and rowed to the moored launch. The skiff would be left on the mooring while the shoreboat was operating. The second shift secured to the mooring after the midnight run and boarded the skiff, now fouled with bird droppings, and approached the pier. I would scramble out and lower the derrick whip wire so the skipper could attach the hoisting sling. Then began laborious cranking on the hand winch until the skiff was level with the pier deck. It was 70 hours a week with no days off, but it paid $60 a month, standard for deckhands at the

Deckhand ready to handle springline.

time. A few worked for less. As a dedicated fisherman I became bored by the monotonous routine and quit after six weeks.

Captain J. H. Andersen successfully operated the Maine-built wooden bark OLYMPIC as a barge at Hermosa Beach from 1926 to 1934. Surviving the frequent winter storms, she eventually rotted away in Cerritos Channel. To replace her Andersen bought the beautiful iron full-rigged ship STAR OF FRANCE and renamed her OLYMPIC II.

The classy ex-clipper was shifted from Hermosa to near the Horseshoe Kelp in 1940. In spite of warnings from the Coast Guard that the heavy traffic area was hazardous, Capt. Andersen kept the location. A productive fishing spot meant good business.

On September 4, 1940 the Japanese steamer SAKITO MARU emerged from thick fog and rammed the barge amidships. Throwing her engines in reverse, the freighter backed away and the sea poured into the damaged barge. OLYMPIC II sank in three minutes with the loss of eight lives.

The use of old windjammer hulls for barges, common for 15 years, was ended by the tragic accident. Sailing ships were generally built with open holds and a single collision bulkhead in the bow. The Bureau of Marine Inspection now decided to enforce a ruling requiring watertight compartments throughout the old hulks. The cost of such extensive alterations would force most barges out of business.

An angry and frustrated Robert Oefinger, owner of the GEORGE E. BILLINGS, declared it was impossible to bring older wooden ships into accord with the federal regulations. Anticipating $500 a day in fines for noncompliance, he determined to cut his losses by destroying BILLINGS. With some fanfare, the big barge was towed out from her winter berth in San Pedro to one of the Channel Islands (probably Santa Barbara) and beached on a rocky shore. On February 10, 1941 she was put to the torch. It was a sorry end for the 37 year old vessel, but a fiery death was perhaps better than creeping deterioration in a stagnant backwater.

A few barges lingered on at their moorings for another year, struggling to survive: FOX, SIERRA and ANNIE M. ROLPH come to mind. The outbreak of war finally finished them off, bringing an end a fascinating chapter in the history of sportfishing.

Aboard the OLYMPIC, 1930.

After the war surplus vessels of all kinds were available and barges again appeared in coastal waters. In general, they had less passenger capacity than the big prewar craft and few survived in business for more than a season. They flourished for a few years while fishing was good, but by 1960 the era of barge fishing was over. Stiff Coast Guard safety requirements, rising overhead and falling patronage combined to finish them off. Fishermen were drawn to fast new party boats that could range far offshore in pursuit of big catches. Stationary barges could no longer compete.

The barge story has not quite ended. A 70-year tradition is carried on today by two barges still in service: ISLE OF REDONDO and ANNIE B. They differ from the oldtimers by being built-for-the-purpose steel vessels designed to conform to strict safety regulations. Similar in shape to the PAPROCA, first of the barges, their flat hulls provide a stable platform for comfortable fishing.

Built at the cost of one million dollars, the 120-foot ISLE OF REDONDO began service in 1980. She rides offshore at the beach city that was the venue over the years for more barges than any other location on the coast. She is sometimes moored over the sunken fishing barge SACRAMENTO, one time San Francisco Bay ferry that went under during a 1968 gale.

ANNIE B. is moored inside the Long Beach breakwater where mackerel, halibut and white croaker are abundant. Frank Hale launched her in 1982 to service fishermen from Belmont and Seal Beach piers. She is similar in design to the ISLE but somewhat smaller being 100 by 50 feet in dimension

A barge trip is a wonderful way to introduce children and skeptical spouses to ocean angling. It is still possible to experience a relaxing day of fishing in a manner enjoyed by thousands during the formative days of sportfishing.

OLYMPIC off Hermosa. Small boat is trolling for barracuda.

STAR OF SCOTLAND, c. 1937.

TWO FISHING STARS

Exploding shells ripped through the hull of the schooner STAR OF SCOTLAND as her startled crew ran for the lifeboats. It was an unlucky Friday the 13th in November of 1942 when the German submarine U-159 trained her deck gun on one of the last American merchant sailing ships to ply her trade. Only six years before her demise in the SouthAtlantic the STAR was peacefully riding at anchor in Santa Monica Bay, serving as a fishing platform for thousands of anglers. When she went down under the U-boat attack she had already outlived a second STAR OF SCOTLAND barge, a former steamship which sank at her moorings off Santa Monica in 1942.

The old windjammer was originally the magnificent four-masted bark KENILWORTH, built of steel at Port Glasgow in 1887 for the British Waverly Line. After nearly twenty years in the Cape Horn trade she was sold to the Alaska Packers Association and renamed STAR OF SCOTLAND. She sailed on annual voyages to the Bering Sea with fishermen and cannery crews, returning with holds full of canned salmon. After a four-year lay up in Oakland Creek she was bought by Charles S. Arnold in 1930 and towed to Santa Monica Bay for service as a sportfishing barge.

After a successful eight year stint as a fishing platform, the big square-rigger, largest of all barges, was sold to gambler Tony Cornero. He stripped her masts and deck fittings and roofed her over, creating a spacious gambling hall. Now called REX, the floating casino was anchored just outside the three mile limit off Santa Monica. Hollywood good-time-charlies and high rollers flocked to REX, generating huge profits for Cornero. However, the prosperity proved to be temporary.

Attorney General Earl Warren became quite annoyed at the offtrack betting and other nefarious activities aboard from which the state collected no tax cut. Officers of the law were sent to close down the REX. A nine-day standoff, known to the press as the "Battle of Santa Monica Bay," ensued with Cornero using fire hoses to repel boarders. The cops at length prevailed and REX was out of business, moldering in the backwaters of Wilmington and seemingly destined for the scrapyard.

The outbreak of war in Europe in 1939 resulted in a shortage of shipping and a rise in freight rates. REX was bought by Frank Hellenthal and partner Charles Lockwood who moved her to Newport Beach for refitting. The former four-masted bark was rerigged as a six-masted schooner and the name REX, never official, was erased.

December 7th, 1941 found the schooner under tow en route to Gray's Harbor for a lumber cargo. After great difficulty Captain Flink obtained a crew and sailed late in January 1942, bound for Cape Town, South Africa. Bad weather and minor damage forced the ship to put in at San Pedro for a brief stay and it was there that she appeared across the slip from the minesweeper in which I was serving. It was a thrill to see her again, even with a much altered rig. I was pleased that once more she was resuming her career as an honorable working vessel.

After a passage of 120 days and a Cape Horn rounding, STAR OF SCOTLAND arrived at Cape Town. Five months later another cargo was fixed for loading in Brazil. She was ten days out from Cape Town when caught by the U-boat that ended her 56-year life in a hail of shellfire.

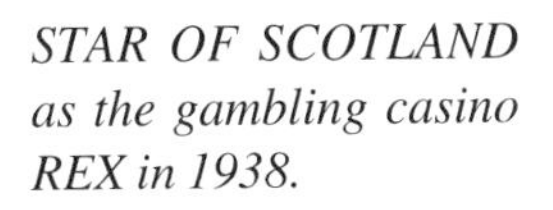

STAR OF SCOTLAND as the gambling casino REX in 1938.

STAR OF SCOTLAND, rerigged as a schooner, departing Gray's Harbor in January, 1942.

Captain Flink and his crew suffered the loss of one man but after ten days in a lifeboat the survivors managed to reach shore in Angola.

To those who remember STAR OF SCOTLAND it is somehow fitting that she "died with her boots on" while tramping the deep sea, doing the work for which she was designed. It was a far better end than rusting away in some stagnant backwater or being torn apart in a wrecker's yard, the fate of a great many fine sailing ships.

The other STAR OF SCOTLAND also had an interesting history, but met a more ignominious end. She, too, had been a gambling ship but when that employment ended she was chartered by the same Charles Arnold that brought the first STAR to Santa Monica. She was the ex-steamship TEXAS but Arnold, intent on reestablishing a once-successful fishing barge operation, attempted to transfer name recognition by calling her STAR OF SCOTLAND. She was fitted with side galleries for fishermen and anchored off Santa Monica where she enjoyed moderate popularity. Arnold's enterprise was short-lived for when war came he turned the vessel back to her owners, W. E. Monstad and Harry Wilson.

The steamer began life as one of the famous British "Q boats" of the first World War. Disguised as harmless merchantmen, the Q boats carried heavy guns hidden behind false bulkheads. Their job was to lure enemy submarines to the surface and sink them with gunfire. After war service

The other STAR OF SCOTLAND, ex-TEXAS, in 1941.

as HMS MISTLETOE, she became CHIAPAS in the freight and passenger trade between California and South America. In the late '20s she was LA PLAYA running "cruises to nowhere" out of Ensenada for thirsty gamblers and party animals. By 1932 she was known as CITY OF PANAMA and later became famous as STAR OF HOLLYWOOD. She finally wound up as the notorious gambling ship TEXAS until deputies of Attorney General Earl Warren raided her on August 1, 1939 and put an end to the business. In 1940 Arnold leased her for use as a floating night club and fishing barge.

The same shipping boom that brought renewed employment to the first STAR brought an offer of $50,000 for the aged steamer. The owners refused it in hopes of greater profit. Dry-docking was planned for the leaky hulk, but due to wartime conditions tug service was not available to haul her into port. The engine was still inside the hull but the propeller had been removed.

On January 23 the leaks suddenly became serious and a desperate struggle began to save the ship. The three crew members summoned Monstad and Wilson who rushed to the barge at 0100 with extra pumps. By 0430 it was clear

OCEANIA VANCE wrecked at Redondo, 1936.

that the sea was winning and the ship was doomed. A flare was fired to summon the lifeguard standing by at the pier. A heavy groundswell was running and the thrust of waves under the fishing galleries apparently lifted a whole row of plates at once for the ship took a sudden plunge and went under in less than two minutes. Drowned was crewman Bill Gillette, but the other four were picked up within minutes by the lifeguard boat and carried to shore. There was no insurance on the sunken vessel.

Thus ended the tale of the two fishing stars. The wreckage of the steamer, now partly buried in the sand, provides a haven and gathering place for all sorts of fish and is a prime angling hot spot for those who know how to find it.

Private boaters can locate the wreck by metering or dragging at a spot approximately one mile from the end of the Santa Monica pier on a heading of 231 degrees magnetic. Depending on the state of the tide, the depth is about 66 feet, or eleven fathoms (see NOAA chart #18744). Drifting the spot is recommended as anchors are often lost in the debris, some of which stands high from the bottom. Rockfish, sculpin and bass are the most frequent catch.

The popularity of the barge-fishing concept is evident when we consider the sheer numbers of vessels employed for the purpose. There were at least 37 former merchant sailing ships and over 60 other types. Many of the latter were simple rectangular scows, but San Francisco Bay ferries, glass-bottom boats, steam lumber schooners, naval landing craft, a kelp harvester, a concrete tow barge, an excursion steamer, an ex-subchaser and a Liberty ship served as well.

Every pier and landing from Santa Barbara to San Diego had one or more barges operating at one time or another. As the barges disappeared so have many of their bases. A number of once-flourishing landings no longer exist. Pine Avenue Pier and Pierpoint in Long Beach are defunct as are the Paradise Cove, Santa Monica, Ocean Park and Venice piers in the Santa Monica Bay. The El Nino-generated waves of 1983 demolished several piers and some were destroyed by fire or deliberate action. Most had long since lost their barge business.

Competition in some areas was intense, notably at Redondo and Long Beach. Many of the barges, especially post-World War II craft, were short-lived, lasting only days, weeks or months before ceasing operations due to misadventure, economic failure or strict Coast Guard regulation. Some changed ownership several times and there was considerable movement in search of profitable locations. By the 1960s barge fishing was finished, not to be revived until ISLE OF REDONDO was launched in 1980.

The appendix contains a list of the known fishing barges culled from newspaper stories, flyers, ads, photos and personal observations. A number are difficult to identify as to hull type. Some duplication is likely as owners often ignored the official registered names and assigned unofficial names for publicity or other reasons. For example MAKAWELI was called RAINBOW and the steam schooner MARTHA BUEHNER was known as the BOUNTY.

Relaxing aboard the NEW POINT LOMA.

A news story on December 12, 1928 tells of the sinking of the "palatial fishing barge BLUE SEA" off San Pedro with the loss of two lives. Listing in the official government record, Merchant Vessels of the U.S., for that name that year is ambiguous. There is some evidence that she was once a Public Health Service fumigation barge. A reported crew of five suggests a sizeable vessel. AILEEN, said to be a barge at Redondo in the 1930s, is not listed under any official classification. It is all very frustrating to a researcher trying to establish accurate data.

Additional information from readers regarding hull types, dates of operation, ownership and other details will be much appreciated by the author.

Formerly the STAR OF FRANCE, the OLYMPIC II is seen here moored off Hermosa Beach in 1934.

A five-ton catch of albacore at Catalina in 1902 furnishes a clue to their abundance.

This 360-pound catch of yellowtail was taken in three hours at Catalina in 1903. Lounging in foreground is Capt. Monty Foster of the launch SUNBEAM.

Part III

THE ABUNDANT FISHES

Chapter 5

THE RIGHT KIND: YELLOWTAIL, TUNA AND DORADO

THE PEOPLE'S FISH

On an April evening in 1934 I was summoned to a friend's home in Santa Monica with the promise that I would see something exceptional. A high school classmate of Japanese extraction had played hooky to join a safari of fishermen making the five-hour trek to exotic San Diego. To my surprise, I was ushered into the family bathroom. Filling the bathtub to the brim was a heap of glistening silver, blue and gold fish. They were yellowtail, glamorous gamesters that at the time I had only dreamed of catching. There were thirty of them, taken at the Coronado Islands on a one-day trip aboard the SEA ANGLER. Fifteen pounds was their average weight.

Excited and envious, I was convinced that the rumors of fantastic fishing to be found at the border city were true. It was indeed possible for a dedicated young angler of limited means to catch big, strong fish as fast as a hook could be baited.

A couple of months later I had my own introduction to the thrill of yellowtail fishing. It was the custom in those Depression days to make the journey south in groups, the riders chipping in all the gas money and sometimes the boat fare of the driver who provided the transportation. After some intensive local fishing and selling the funds were accumulated to finance a trip. The boat fare was $3 and the gas money was $2. A regular on the Santa Monica boats, known to me only as "Ace," provided the vehicle, a sort of primitive panel truck used in his painting business. There were four of us in the group. It was a long, bumpy ride, but youthful anticipation made light of discomfort.

We fished from Frank Kiessig's SPORTFISHER. Fitted to my handwrapped bamboo rod was a Pflueger "Ohio" reel filled with green 12-thread linen line. A three-foot wire leader with attached 2/0 O'Shaughnessy hook completed the rig. I hooked my first ever yellow with a trolled sardine as the boat made a chum circle off Pukey Point. I landed it too, along with six others including a 20-pounder. The fishing

Fishing in the Golden Years: Sept. 6, 1933, 32 anglers on SPORTFISHER capture a record 322 yellowtail.

was considered to be only fair. I lost a couple, including a sizeable tuna, but all in all it was a satisfactory trip, the first of many to come. From then on I considered myself a seasoned yellowtail fisherman.

On the same trip was another group travelling in the stake truck owned by a local fish merchant. He was considered to be "hungry" and somewhat miserly in his dealings with fishermen. During the peak of the yellowtail bite he put up his rod and rushed to the middle of the stern with a ball of heavy handline. He caught one fish, horsing it in and bouncing it in the commercial manner. As he went to the tank for another bait, the deckhand tossed the handline overboard, much to the amusement of those who knew the greedy one. Handline and jackpole fishing were widespread along the coast, but on Kiessig's boats only rod-and-reel fishing was allowed.

Charles Frederick Holder, the founding father and learned guru of ocean sportfishing, described yellowtail as the "fish of the people." He declared that men, women and children, everyone who fished in fact, tried for them and none could resist the appeal of their gameness and beauty. He first encountered yellowtail, also known as white salmon and amberfish, on a visit to Catalina in 1886. He wrote: "Men and boys were standing on the beach catching yellowtails with cod handlines. As fast as they could cast, they had strikes. The fish ranged from 20 to 35 pounds in weight, and every few minutes there would be a wailing and gnashing of teeth as a yellowtail would break the ropes they were fishing with."

An inspired Holder busted a lot of tackle, but eventually took countless yellowtail on rod and reel. He went on to catch a variety of big game species, but always retained a special fondness for the amber beauties. In his 1906 book, *The Log of a Sea Angler*, he states: "No fish exceeds it in game or fighting qualities, and I have never seen a yellowtail hooked that did not make a heroic fight. The yellowtail never gives in; it never knows that it is caught."

San Diego's fame as a sportfishing center was founded on the excellence and consistency of nearby yellowtail fishing. The local newspaper reported a 1935 total of over 100,000 yellowtail and 13,000 tuna. New records were set by San Diego boats in 1936. For example: on May 12 SPORTFISHER II made a catch of 546 yellowtail 17 to 18 pounds for 46 anglers. On May 17 Capt. Bill Miller of the STAR ANGLER claimed an all-time Sunday record when his 35 passengers landed 623 yellowtail. Not every year was a bonanza. In 1939 the yellowtail catch was "only" 58,000!

My diary for March 18, 1938 tells of a trip to the Coronados on Nick Johns' AZTEC. A huge ground swell and choppy sea wiped out most of the anglers with seasickness. The water was yellow-brown and we fished on the bottom with heavy sinkers. At 0900 the bite switched on and my partner and I dredged up 21 yellows between us. The boat total was 167 fish. They were what we called "firecrackers"—fish averaging 12 to 15 pounds each. We hauled them up to Santa Monica in the rumble seat of the Model A Ford coupe and peddled them to Ralph's market for ten cents a pound cleaned, heads on. After a day's rest we again headed for San Diego—about four hours driving along old Highway 101. The fishing wasn't quite as good, but we still made a profit. Total expenses for both of us, including fares for two days of fishing and gas for the car, came to only $14!

Fishing at the Coronado Islands, Catalina and other locations no longer offers the consistency and volume of those times, but whenever they are in a biting mood yellowtail never fail to attract hordes of anglers. They are still the fish of the people.

John Raymond caught this record 53-3 yellowtail at Catalina in 1919.

These primly dressed customers of Avalon guide Washburn pose with 1901 albacore. Bait was fresh dead sardines or smelt.

ALBACORE

California sportfishermen have been pursuing albacore, with more or less intensity, for at least one hundred years. The longfins were at first not highly regarded as food and commercial fishermen considered them a downright nuisance.

Anglers with the resources to charter a launch made some fabulous hauls. Charles Frederick Holder wrote in 1909 that albacore could be found near the Channel Islands almost any week of the year. "I believe no fish in these waters will so impress the stranger; not only for their vast numbers, but for their extraordinary tameness."

The chief fishing area, Holder states, was two miles directly off Avalon. Once there, trolling was unnecessary. The launch was allowed to drift as the boatman chummed with dead sardines or cut bait. The albacore would soon appear as a ravenous horde, taking everything that was tossed over. He writes: "To test their tameness, impale a sardine on your gaff and lower it down. In a moment a thirty-pounder has seized it and you have gaffed him and lifted him in. But I advise you not to tell the story, as no one will believe it, though it is one of the easiest things to accomplish when these fishes are biting in their normal fashion."

Evidence of the superabundance of fish is to be found in the chapter heading photo. The original caption says it is a five-ton catch of albacore taken in a half day's fishing with rods and reels. Nearly 200 fish are visible hanging from the racks and more are heaped on the ground. As the picture is cropped at the edges the total probably exceeded the 237 I was able to count. The fish are in the 30 to 40-pound range and 250 of them would indeed add up to five tons.

Twenty-one smug sports and crewmen are posing with the mighty haul. Twelve rods are visible, each with its knuckle-buster reel. Conforming to the custom of the times, the lucky anglers are attired in suits, fedora hats and neckties. The boatmen wear seamen's caps and are tieless. Some are holding gaffs.

Also remarkable is that this fantastic slaughter must have been made at a very short distance from Avalon. The charter boats then at the island were slow open launches about 20 feet long, usually carrying not more than two passengers. Rods were mostly of wood and reels had only thumb drags and clickers. Bait would have been salted or fresh dead. Talk about your wide open bites--it must have been almost beyond belief! The obvious effort that went into assembling all the fish, racks and people in one location to pose for the photo indicates an exceptional catch even for those days.

Partyboat sportfishing for albacore in early times was mostly by trolling. Operating from Long Beach in 1918, a few boats were fitted with long outrigger poles and commercial-type jig lines. The poles, each dragging six lines, were rigged out from the sides. Twelve passengers sat on benches, six to a side, and over his shoulder each held a pull-in line leading to one of the jig lines. When a strike was felt the fisherman would stand up and haul in his fish hand over hand. To have an equal chance with the most productive lines, anglers would rotate their places on the bench after each catch. In addition to the handliners, four others trolled from the stern with heavy rods and reels. The jigs were chummed with salt bait.

Maurice Schipper with nice Coronados bluefin in 1932. Note knuckle-buster reel and large hook.

Col. C. P. Morehouse poses with his 251-pound tuna. This fish held the Catalina record from 1899 to 1983.

TUNA TALES

Long ago, as a boy learning to fish, I yearned to catch a bluefin tuna. Although I had no expectations of conquering any but a smaller specimen, it seemed the most prestigious prize I could take. Sharing the "tuna experience," even in a very small way, with such angling giants as C. F. Holder and Zane Grey would be exciting enough in my youthful imagination.

My first tuna was sacked on a trip to the Coronados in 1935. School bluefin were common at the islands then, 13,000 being taken there that year. After losing several, I was thrilled to bring in a 32-pounder.

Partially accounting for the large numbers of tuna captured by the San Diego boats was the steady availability of sardines. The large baits swam almost naturally even when towing a wire leader and linen line. With the tackle then in use hooking bluefin on anchovies was a tough proposition, akin in difficulty to catching wild trout on a dry fly. Extremely hook-shy in the clear water, small tuna were present around Catalina long after the big trophy sizes had vanished.

With the switch to monofilament lines in the 1950s the catch of bluefin on anchovy baits rose dramatically, over 34,000 being caught on partyboats in 1956, the peak year. My personal score also improved with top one-day scores on 'chovies of six in 1953 and eleven in 1973. They are still my favorite angling target.

Although they occasionally bite without caution, particularly when schooling with albacore, inducing such spooky critters to strike is especially challenging. A light line, tiny hook and above all a lively bait are starting requirements for bluefin fishing. They can be taken by trolling, but are least likely of all the tunas to be caught on jigs. In the old days sports hung the big ones on trolled flying fish and after 1909 increased their success by using kites to skip the bait in a natural manner.

Holder and Grey both wrote colorful accounts of the enormous schools of tuna found around the Channel Islands before the seiners found a way to catch them. It was the bluefin's habit to drive flying fish before them within the horns of a shallow arc perhaps a mile or more across. Churning up a surf of white water hundreds of giant tuna soared through the air as they pursued the fleeing flyers. It was such rousing scenes that caused Holder to apply the name "leaping tuna" to the great fish.

Only once did I see anything like it on a large scale, although the fish were smaller. It was on the Horseshoe Kelp in 1937 where a fleet of commercial and sport boats was working barracuda. A huge school of frantic anchovies suddenly rushed past chased by acres and acres of feeding tuna. Right through the fleet the frenzied tuna charged, jumping and crashing everywhere, while excited anglers presented baits as expertly as they knew how. What frustration! No exultant shouts were heard and nowhere did I see a bent rod. As far as I could tell not one of the thousands of feeding bluefin took a hook.

In 1910 G.A. Murphy bested this 175-pounder after a two hour and 15 minute struggle.

BLUEFIN COMEBACK

A catch of giant bluefin tuna at Guadalupe Island in 1986 caused a stir of excitement along the South Coast. Tuna of 298, 203 and 135 pounds were taken from the six-pac boat PEARL skippered by Tom Moreno. Other large bluefins have been caught in recent years, notably the 363 1/2 pound record-breaker snared by Newport angler Jim Salter in 1983. Long range sportfishers have frequently spotted the huge tuna at Guadalupe, but they usually stay clear of the big boats. Even so, a 279-pounder was taken by Dick Cresswell from the NEW RED ROOSTER in July 1982. Fishing from an inflatable rubber raft, Tom McMillan of Newport Beach landed a 250-pound tuna at the island and a 398-pounder was captured by a spearfisherman.

Outsize bluefin tuna in waters accessible to California anglers launched big game fishing as a sport back in 1898 when Charles Frederick Holder boated a 183-pounder on rod and reel off Catalina. The following year Col. C. P. Morehouse took one of 251 pounds that stood as a record for 84 years, until Salter's catch.

Holder went on to found the world famous Tuna Club at Avalon and his writings did much to stimulate public interest in sportfishing. He was a tireless advocate of marine conservation and was instrumental in getting legislation passed in 1913 declaring Catalina a preserve off limits to commercial netting.

Although the number had been declining since 1918 when purse seiners found a way to capture them, large fish over 100 pounds continued to be caught on rod and reel until the early 1930s. For nearly 50 years big tuna were absent from local waters, but it now appears they may be on the verge of a comeback. If the fish reappear in any numbers it can be anticipated that modern tackle and methods will hook and land more of the giants than in old times.

Holder called the big bluefins "leaping tuna" for their tendency to clear the water when feeding. Painting by the author.

Clad in his corduroy fishing suit, Charles F. Holder admires his 183-pound bluefin. Jim Gardner is the guide.

In Holder's day big fish were caught with knuckle buster reels and linen lines from small launches putting around in the calm waters of Catalina Island's lee side. It was no pastime for sissies. Fighting large tuna on primitive tackle could be traumatic and one angler dislocated his arm during a contest. Another "dropped senseless in the boat" as his 180 pound prize came to gaff after a five-hour battle. Exhaustion, cramps, broken knuckles and cut, battered hands were commonplace when battling tuna.

Holder's favorite bluefin fishing tale (mine, too) began when a 95-pounder was gaffed aboard the skiff from which he, a companion, and his boatman, Jim Gardner, were fishing. The fish, still "green," sprang into the air and fell on the gunwale, overturning the boat. In the excitement of being dunked, Holder dropped his expensive rod and gave it up for lost as he swam toward a nearby launch. His companion, who could not swim, clung to the overturned skiff. Holder's waterlogged corduroy suit, leggings and heavy shoes so weighed him down that two men in the launch could not drag him aboard. Pending the arrival of additional help, he was tied to the rigging.

Meanwhile, the gaffer Gardner, who was known to be a good swimmer, was seen bobbing erratically up and down and it was feared he was being attacked by sharks. He had never released his hold on the gaff, which was still impaled in the struggling tuna, and the fish kept pulling him under. Aided by the launch crew, Holder was finally able to get his hand in the fish's gills and, after much ado, he and it were hauled aboard.

A happy "hot stick" shows off his catch of 18 yellows on the SAN ANTONIO.

After rescuing Gardner and the man clinging to the skiff, the boat was righted, floating gear was recovered, and the launch headed for Avalon. Gardner suddenly clutched at his pants and hollered for the boat to stop. Snagged in his trousers was the hook that had caught the tuna, until this time unnoticed in the excitement. Seeing that its leader led overboard, he began hauling and pulled up 600 feet of line and the still attached rod and reel. Holder was delighted by the adventure and later wrote, "I have not claimed the Carnegie hero medal for my boatman, but all anglers will appreciate the cleverness and nerve of this man in saving his patron's fish under what, to put it mildly, were adverse circumstances."

T. Robustus

BIG EYE, BIG FISH

Possessing characteristics of each, bigeye tuna have always appeared to me to be a cross between yellowfin and albacore. With the coloring of yellowfin they wear long pectoral fins and large eyes similar to albacore. A thorough scientific description of the Pacific strain was made in 1923 by Tokyo biologist Kishinouye who dubbed them *Parathunnus mebachi*, the latter word meaning "big eye" in Japanese. Although occasional catches were made by U.S. fishermen they were always lumped with yellowfin in fish reports. Little effort was made to separate them until recent years. The all-out offshore pursuit of albacore by sportfishermen brought more frequent contact with bigeyes. They are the large tuna most likely to be caught on short-range local trips.

Scientific boffins now use the Latin name *Thunnus obesus*, which means simply "fat tuna," for this noble fish. I don't care for the implication of overweight sluggishness in that designation. If the professor who dreamed that up had ever been one-on-one with a large bigeye hooked on rod and reel, I dare say he would have thought of something more appropriate. *T. robustus* or *T. potens*, meaning strong or powerful, would be more like it!

SPORTS CAR TUNA

My first encounter with yellowfin tuna came in 1936 aboard Schipper & Sons' boat REX. Engine trouble prevented our arrival at the hot area until late in the day. A vast thrashing boil of tuna was foaming at the shallow Middle Grounds of the Coronado Islands. A fast-running strike came within moments of my first cast with a sardine bait. Adrenaline surged as I swung my rod for hookset. In a millisecond the bight of slack linen line sprang taut, flinging a shower of bright drops in the air. With a prolonged, snake-like hiss the line cut the surface water at incredible speed. In the time it took to flip the reel in gear the fish crossed the boat's bow and raced far out to starboard. The bait had been taken on the port quarter, but luckily there were few passengers and my mad dash to the bow was unimpeded. That first wild run of my first yellowfin tuna is still a treasured memory, fresh and vivid. On that wonderful day I went on to land four tuna and three skipjack along with five yellowtail, an outstanding catch at any time.

Yellowfin are to me the most handsome of the tuna family, a racy sports car-type fish. I like their bright fins, golden side stripes and the silver spots and marks that show on their bellies when fresh from the water. It's exciting to watch them darting back and forth as they gobble bait in the clear depths, their brownish backs easily distinguishable from the electric-blue skipjack .

Most of all I like their tendency to go on feeding frenzies, berserk behavior equalled only by skipjack. They don't always bite with abandon, but on the average are much easier to hook than bluefin. It seems also that they frequently carry on their thrilling fights more toward the surface than other tunas. They are the mainstay of long range fishing.

A marvelous run of yellowfin tuna developed off San Diego in the fall of 1936. It was similar to the fishing in 1992 except that the fish were found even closer inshore. Big catches of tuna and skipjack were taken at the close-in Coronado Islands by boats on 10-hour, one day trips. No need for high speed, all night cruising to distant offshore banks to find fish.

Some typical catches: On September 2, 1936, Star & Crescent's boat VIRGINIA brought back 16 anglers with a catch of 32 yellowfin and 103 yellowtail. STAR ANGLER had 32 tuna, 65 yellows and a dolphin. Twenty-four on SEA ANGLER caught 33 yellowtail, five bluefin and 39 yellowfin. The tuna scaled between 20 and 30 pounds. On the 8th, SEA ANGLER returned with 91 yellowfin and 10 yellowtail. Many skipjack were taken, but not included in the counts. It got better.

Nine fishermen on H & M's MASCOT II sacked 77 yellowfin averaging 24 pounds on September 21. Dewey Hartman of San Dimas was "hot stick" with 14 fish and R. B. Johnson took ten. It was still going strong in October when 25 sports landed 41 tuna and 56 skipjack. A. Z. England of San Pedro caught 10 tuna and L. E. Brady of Colton boated six including a 23-pounder.

It is depressing that really good tuna fishing is now rarely experienced in near-shore waters as it was in the old days (with the exception of the 1992 run). My belief is that the cumulative effect of massive pollution has tainted coastal waters. The great migrations of albacore and tuna to the Coronado Islands and the Catalina Channel no longer occur as they once did. A few brave stragglers wander in each year, but not the millions of fish that once came our way. The waning of inside runs corresponds to the pace of population growth and the increase of wastes dumped into the ocean. Sedentary species living in coastal areas have been able to adjust gradually to changing conditions, but the true pelagic fishes tolerate only pure, clean water. Sadly, it seems that the situation will never be reversed and it is likely that we will have to travel ever further offshore to find our tuna favorites.

WARM WATER DAYS

In 1937 exotics swarmed in coastal waters. Off San Diego the SPORTFISHER II, skippered by Mel Shears, made a one-day, one-boat haul of over 600 dorado. At the time anglers made the bulk of their catches close to shore and most were unfamiliar with dolphinfish. It was an El Nino year, but Californians were not yet familiar with the term. We were delighted that a warm water cycle was generating fantastic catches of rare gamefish.

A rare catch of dorado at Santa Monica, 1928.

My partner and I decided to check out the new (for us) type of fishing. We got out on a gorgeous day of calm seas and blue waters. A fleet of commercial boats was working over schools of skipjack and yellowfin tuna in an area only a few miles off Pt. Loma. The first stop on a kelp paddy was sensational. Wild action was instant as the dorados went into their maypole dance around the boat, their runs and leaps weaving lines over and under. The golden beauties repeated the spectacle numerous times that memorable day. Small tuna also came our way when I hooked up while trolling a sardine through a school of breaking fish.

That evening we stowed the fish in the rumble seat of the Model A Ford and took off for L.A. to peddle our catch. To our dismay the small markets and restaurants on our route refused to buy. None had ever seen a dolphin or heard of the Hawaiian taste treat, mahi-mahi. Spoilage was imminent and it was time for desperate measures if the fish were not to be lost.

Noticing that the golden dorado tails protruding from the crushed ice in our fish box bore a close resemblance to the caudal fins of yellowtail, I had an inspiration. If we removed the heads of our fish they appeared similar to cleaned yellowtail, albeit more silvery and with much flatter sides. Chop, chop and back into the ice went the dolphins minus their funny-looking heads. They were quickly disposed of at yellowtail prices. One buyer remarked on the flat bodies, but I told him it was a result of the fish being well packed down in the ice.

A few days later we were again touring our customer outlets with another load of dorados. One fellow bought the entire lot. He had discovered how delicious the dolphin meat was in the frying pan and was serving it to his restaurant patrons as a featured "yellowtail" dish. However, he insisted on paying less because, as he put it, "I don't know what these things are, but they're not yellowtail—they are flat as boards!"

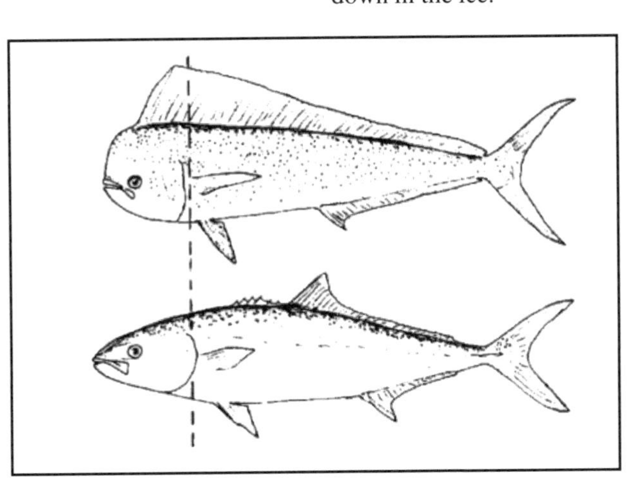

Dolphinfish and yellowtail.

A GOLDEN TROPHY

A hundred yards from the boat a bull dolphin cleared the back of a blue swell and caught the glint of early sun on his broad golden side before plunging back in a shower of spray. "What a moose! I wonder who has him hooked?" The thought flashed through my mind as I concentrated on deciding which way to dip my rod in an attempt to thread a way through a thicket of bent poles.

It was Sunday, August 25, 1957. A fishing pal and I, along with 58 other eager souls, had sailed from San Diego aboard the POLARIS. We accepted the certainty of tangled lines and other frustrations inherent in full-load party fishing in order to sample the fantastic fishing that was prevalent during a warm water cycle.

After fast and furious dawn action near North Coronado Island my sack held four yellowtail. When the bite tapered off Skipper Bill Poole hollered, "Wind 'em up! We'll take a run outside and see if we can find some dolphin." As we headed offshore Poole kept a sharp lookout for patches of floating kelp or other debris under which dorado assemble.

After a 30 minute cruise the first kelp paddy was spotted and the deckhand tossed chum as we pulled up to the drifting weeds. First hookups came before the boat was finally stopped. Rather than cast over the crisscrossing lines farther out I dropped a lively green-backed anchovy straight down off the stern and fed out line. When the small rubber-core sinker had pulled the bait a few yards under I felt a strike and set the hook. Line sizzled from the reel as I tried to follow the fish. It was only seconds later that I first saw the big dorado silhouetted against the sky.

Everywhere hooked dolphin were bouncing over the sea in a mad dance around the boat. Excited anglers ran, stumbled, elbowed and cursed in a frantic scramble to follow their fish and keep free from tangles. In the thick of this wild melee I again raised the tip of my long fiberglass rod in what I hoped was the right direction and suddenly, miraculously, my line whipped clear of the spaghetti-like web of snarled monofilament. It led far out over the surface, clear of the mess at boatside. Once again the 9-foot stick proved its worth for party boat fishing as I backed off and passed its arc high over the rods at the rail.

Working my way after the hissing line, I followed toward the bow. Once out of the worst confusion I settled down to subdue the powerful fish I had hooked. Much 20-pound test mono had melted from the reel while fighting clear of the tangles, and I watched anxiously as more yards peeled off.

A Golden Trophy.

Again a bright flash of gold, green and cobalt blue as a fish leaped far away. Five times he flung himself in the air, and I could see he was a large one. Was it the bull I had spotted earlier? It now seemed likely since most of the other hookups had by now been lost or brought to gaff. Still my fish was slow to yield.

The skipper had spotted another kelp paddy a few hundred yards off and was urging me to hurry. All kinds of advice and encouragement were offered by the other anglers, who by now were mere spectators. Ignoring it all, I concentrated on keeping cool and letting my tackle work for me.

At last, after tense minutes, steady pumps gained line and the great fish was alongside. No need to shout, "Color!" Two gaffers already stood by. Planing away with his boardlike body, the dolphin made his last tired run and a feeble attempt to jump. It was a dying effort. In short order the gaff sank home and the prize was mine.

It was difficult to keep my gaze from the magnificent creature. There is no more beautiful fish in the sea than dorado and it was my largest to that time. The average weight of those taken was around eight pounds, but mine weighed in at 27 pounds, 12 ounces. Not a real giant as dorado go, he was nevertheless exceptional among those babies. Many more dolphin have come my way over the years, including some larger, but none matched the thrill of that particular catch. He was the best fish of the trip, the season, and the year. Among thousands of many species caught in a lifetime of dedicated fishing, that bull dorado is my golden trophy.

Slaughter of yellowtail at Catalina, c. 1905.

Founding fathers of the world-famous Tuna Club of Avalon, June 1898. Holder, second from right, was instigator and first president.

Herring were favorite baits. From a painting by the author.

Bull bass slaughter in the days of no limits.

Chapter 6
THE THREE B'S: BASS, BARRACUDA AND BONITO

POPULAR INDIVIDUALS

Before 1954 a top item on the seafood menu of many restaurants was a dish called "individual rock bass." It consisted of a kelp or sand bass cooked with the head on and served whole in the manner of rainbow trout. Ten to twelve inch fish fit nicely on a platter. Bass of that size were always in demand and brought a premium price. Large fish that required filleting sold for less. The pressure on juveniles was doubtless detrimental to the resource and probably was a factor in the eventual removal of the species from the marketplace.

A good deal of partyboat fishing time, then as now, was spent trying for bass. Backing right into the heart of a thick kelp bed was one way to get good results. Hanging up in the weeds was less worrisome when linen lines and wire leaders were the normal rig. Aside from rod and reel, one way to hook a mess of marketable individuals was to poke a hole through the kelp with a gaff and drop in a three or four-hook handline baited with pinheads. Nor was it unusual for anglers using long jackpoles to drop a bait straight down into honey holes not easily accessible with rod and reel.

The favorite bait for bull bass (over three pounds) was herring (Queenfish, *Seriphus politus*) or brown bait as it is called today. Horse sardines were also productive, but being extra lively had a tendency to wrap around the kelp. Live squid were unavailable. There were no specialized artificial lures for ocean bass, but some sporty fellows occasionally used fresh water plugs with good results. Barracuda feathers also worked fairly well.

The largest bass I ever landed was a 13-pounder, a purple, green and gold giant wrestled from the Point Dume kelp in 1933. Wrenched from my grip by the bull's first lunge, the handle of my dragless reel whirred backwards, painfully lashing my knuckles. Swallowing the large herring bait in a gulp, the huge bass dashed through the weeds, boring into the heart of the kelp forest. When the fish was solidly wrapped, the skipper coached me to take a heavy strain on the line and twang it like a banjo string. The vibrations were calculated to stir the sulking fish into motion. The twanging was followed by complete slack to allow the bass some movement, hopefully in a new direction leading out of the mesh of weeds. When activity was detected the slack was taken up and the fish horsed strongly to head it toward the boat. After some lengthy give and take the big bass, festooned with kelp, was close enough to gaff. This technique for working bass through the kelp is just as effective today as it was sixty years ago.

Check the size of some of these bass caught on RAMONA.

Department of Fish & Game official nomenclature was slightly different then. The fish now labeled sand bass was officially rock bass, but to anglers they were ground bass. The official kelp bass was a calico, as to many it still is. There was a good deal of confusion, then as now, with olive rockfish, often miscalled "Johnny bass." Their resemblance to real bass compounds the identity problem.

The commercial catch of bass averaged around 500,000 pounds a year until 1940, but declined rapidly after WW II. Sixty-nine percent of the take was on hook and line. About 20 percent was taken in traps and the rest in nets. I once helped a trap fisherman pull his gear and in addition to a lot of sand bass, the chicken wire trap contained small rockfish, sculpin and hordes of beautiful red and blue rainbow perch. In 1932 the total catch was about 87 percent kelp bass and 13 percent sand bass. Spotted bass, found mostly in bays, were an insignificant part of the catch and usually lumped with sand bass. Removing bass from the market and imposing the 12 inch size limit was neither too little nor too late. Consistent catches of sizeable fish , in spite of tremendous fishing pressure, are proof of the relatively healthy state of the resource. After rockfish and mackerel, bass are the third most numerous catch on sportboats.

These formally dressed lads reeled in these barries near Avalon, c. 1902.

APPRECIATING BARRACUDA

In a 1931 study of barracuda it was found that fish of larger size were taken at the Channel Islands than along the coast. In my commercial trolling days I often fished island waters and I don't remember ever catching shorts out there. Sportfishermen came to expect the big ones around the isles and referred to them as "Catalina stovepipes." Eight to twelve-pounders were common.

It has been a long time since I've seen a 12-pound barracuda, let alone caught one. They are not often found in retail stores, even though they remain a legal commercial target. Over fishing and other causes reduced this once-plentiful species to the point where it is seldom pursued as a market fish. Most seafood consumers have long lost the habit of eating barries.

Ocean Park anglers proudly display catch of barries.

Barracuda figured prominently in the commercial and sport catch from the very beginnings of those industries. As late as 1968 they were considered by sportfishing operators to be the most important species overall, followed by bass and yellowtail. A government report dated 1889 states that barracuda fishing off San Diego was carried out by one or two men in small sailboats and that the quantity caught varied greatly from day to day according to the wind. "The greatest number caught by two men in one boat in a day was 1,100. They can only be caught by trolling and a light wind brings few fish. Many barracuda are now salted and shipped." Another report tells of an enormous school of barracuda some twenty acres in extent that lingered in the area from San Pedro to Santa Monica in the early part of the present century.

An inkling of their abundance and the rate of unregulated waste and destruction that took place in the bad old days may be had from the official notes of the California Fish & Game Commission for 1919. On April 30, the net boat MINNIE F. brought in 58,995 pounds of barracuda, all of which were pulverized in a reduction plant. The barries in the photo of the 29-ton catch all appear to be logs of eight or nine pounds.

Note the size of these "Catalina stovepipes."

In 1920 the commercial catch of barracuda exceeded eight million pounds, mostly taken in purse seines and round haul nets. It has been downhill ever since, although tonnage remained above two million pounds through the 1940s. Catches gradually dwindled until the commercial fishery practically ceased and sports took mostly undersized fish.

One of the most effective methods of catching barracuda in the '30s was to cast a small feather jig and retrieve it with a fast stop-start crank. It was much favored by teenage anglers intent on taking the maximum number of fish for later peddling. Those that practiced the method became known as "feather merchants."

A feather merchant bounces a snake aboard the barge NEW POINT LOMA.

In the time between the world wars barracuda were available as food everywhere in Southern California and were especially popular during the Depression years. Sizeable, marketable, plentiful and easy to catch, they were favorites of the "kid commercials" and "feather merchants."

On some boats it was possible to keep barries straight as rigor mortis set in by stowing them in a sack laid flat under the bench seats. This was important as fish in hanging sacks often assumed a horseshoe shape. The flesh becomes mushy when the curl is forcibly straightened. To prevent fresh-caught scooters from flopping out of the sack it was customary to kill them quickly by clubbing with a piece of pipe or other

Chanting, "Gotta make my fare back!" a feather merchant works his lure in a rhythmic stop and start retrieve.

heavy object. Sometimes they were strung on a rope and dropped over the side and catches were sometimes lost when fishermen failed to haul stringers aboard before the boat got underway.

On modern party boats the sacks are hung on hooks around the tank or on the rail. To keep a "snake" straight and in prime condition put a small loop of mono line around the tail and suspend the fish from a sack hook, bleeding it at the same time. Barracuda are best for eating when the blood lines on each side of the body are removed and the meat marinated in milk. They are tasty when fried, barbecued, broiled or baked. They are also excellent when smoked.

Commercial methods of barracuda fishing are covered in Chapter 9.

BONITO, THE POOR MAN'S TUNA

Bonito were not always held in the high esteem they now enjoy. In the old days they were seldom targeted by boat fishermen and were derided as "Laguna tuna," considered only slightly more desirable than mackerel. They were, however, favorites with pier and barge anglers.

When I was a boy making my first expeditions to the Santa Monica pier, bonito were taken with regularity. If I could catch one I felt it would be a sign that I had graduated from "perch picker" to full-fledged saltwater fisherman. Trouble was, I lacked proper tackle.

After ruining my Dad's trout tackle, I bought a 50-yard spool of standard linen line meant for use on a reel. It was nearly useless as a handline but I was stuck with it. Much of

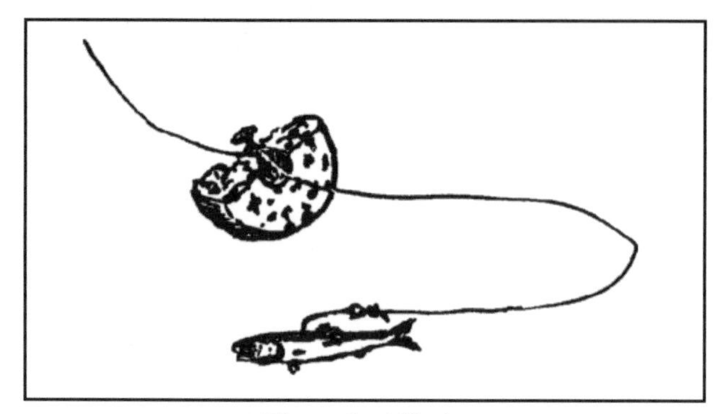

The makeshift rig.

my precious fishing time was spent untangling the soft cord. I had no gut or wire leaders and my hooks were miniature size 12 and 14 suitable only for perch.

Three-pound bonito swarmed around the pier on a summer day and rod-and-reel and jackpole anglers were easily hooking up. Some were casting cork splashers and feather jigs and others were using live bait. I wished desperately to catch one of the speedy fighters, but without the proper rig I had little chance.

Scrounging around the pier I found an old Kirby hook about size 2, half a broken net cork, and a large rusty nail. The hook was fastened to the end of my linen line with three half-hitches. The nail was pushed through the cork and the makeshift float was tied about two feet above the hook. Precious pennies were spent on a few live anchovies and I baited up and made my handline cast. Bonito were clearly visible darting about and boiling on the surface. A couple of my minnows were knocked off without a hookup. It was nearly impossible to set the hook through the slack handline. The rest of the anchovies expired in the coffee can before I could use them.

Up and over the rail.

Except for my carfare home, only a nickel was left and with it I got a few more live baits. They too, were expended without results. Just one remained. It was impaled through the middle of the back and tossed in. The anchovy, held up by the cork, fluttered feebly near the surface. Almost choking with tension and frustration, I watched intently as several "boneheads" made swift passes at my last-chance bait. Suddenly a bonito charged, the cork was yanked under and the line went taught! I hauled back instinctively and had my first bonito on the hook.

Hand over hand it came up and over the rail to the deck. There never lived a happier or prouder angler than I as I fell upon my flopping prize. It was the largest fish of any kind that I had yet captured and the thrill of that great moment is as clear in my memory today as it was all those many moons ago.

The perch I caught during the balance of the day were not kept. Nothing was going to detract from the triumph of the first bonito. Left exposed for all passersby to admire, its skin wrinkled after hours in the hot sun and the meat began to turn mushy. Nevertheless, I bore it home and presented it to my parents who dutifully praised and cooked it. It was less than gourmet fare, but to me it tasted absolutely marvelous.

Whether or not anglers find them desirable as food bonito rank high as game fish. When it comes to fighting ability a ten-pound bonito is the equal of any albacore of the same size. It is regrettable that the larger boneheads over five pounds are not more plentiful. They furnish prime sport whenever they are available.

Morris boat deckhands Jimmy Grant and Otmar Bethel hold gigantic 22-pound bonito. Boneheads of this size are rare indeed.

Two of the Three B's: bass and barracuda, are strung up by this old timer.

Note size of bull bass in lower right. Catch made at Oceanside, 1938.

Capt. McKay and friends hooked these logs and a yellowtail at Catalina in 1919.

Young "merchants" show off their score of scooters. Sign advertises fishing on Redondo barge IRENE for $1.

Eager bystanders try to get into the act with this 427-pound giant black seabass caught from Hermosa Pier in 1921.

Giant totuava, cousin to the white seabass, were once plentiful in the Sea of Cortez.

Chapter 7
CATALINA SALMON AND OCEAN HIPPOS

Catching a white seabass was once a not unreasonable expectation. Fishing near an offshore island, in a kelp bed or at night from a pier increased the chance of success. At the turn of the century huge schools of fifty-pounders cruised the shores of Catalina and the island is still a favorite haunt of the big croakers. One of the local names for the great fish was "Catalina salmon." Slow trolling along the edge of the kelp with a large Wilson spoon was a productive technique at the island. The spoon's violent flashing wobble simulates the large mouthful that seems irresistible to seabass. Avalon anglers also did well on summer nights trolling flying fish baits.

In the 1930s Newport Pier was the center of activity during the dark of the moon phase each May. Hooking large bass from 20 to 50 pounds was commonplace. In Santa Monica Bay the best pier fishing seemed to be in the fall when dense schools of sardines gathered around the pilings. Serious fishermen lowered hooded Coleman lanterns close to the water to attract and concentrate the 'deens. Bait caught by snagging was offered on a flyline or lightly sinkered rig. The surface splash of massed sardines leaping together was a sure sign that seabass were on the prowl. Although plentiful, pier-caught bass were usually juveniles. Everyone called them "sea trout."

Amazingly, small sea trout will attack baits nearly their own size. Once, while fishing at the Barn Kelp for giant black seabass, I caught a greedy little five-pound white that attacked a live mackerel pinned to a 12/0 hook. Somehow it managed to inhale the 2-pound mac and huge hook without dislocating its jaw.

My best-ever catch of white seabass came at San Onofre on Labor Day, 1941. On holiday from the navy, I was there on the SUNSHINE II out of King's Landing. Dirty water and offshore wind seemed to indicate poor fishing.

To my surprise, someone hauled up a small white seabass. Already tied to my line was a chrome-plated Dodger jig. As skipper Sammy Cordeiro brailed out the chum, I began to yo-yo the lure a few feet from the bottom. After two "yos" the line went slack. On the next upswing the rod bent double to the heavy, throbbing resistance that signals a solid hookup. My arms jolting to the typical rattling head-shake of a white seabass, I hot-railed around the boat. After a due amount of give and take my prize came belly-up to the gaff, a nice 20-pounder. No giant of the species, but no peanut, either.

During the course of that super day I piled the deck

The noble croaker.

with 14 more identical to the first, all on the Dodger. It turned out that I had the only jig aboard. As the bait was entirely pinheads the shiny lure was just what it took to get the attention of the hungry whites. The others got a fish or two on the small bait, but none could match me for quick hookups and big fish. I've caught a good many since then, some of them large fish, but always with decreasing frequency and numbers.

Before the 1880s the commercial fishery for white seabass was centered in the San Francisco-Monterey area. An apparent change in hydrographic conditions led to disappearance of the fish in the north and they have never returned in any significant numbers. In the 1920s large schools could be surrounded with purse seines and lampara nets and slaughtered by the ton. This fishery was carried on at night and the nets were set on "fireballs" of phosphorescence marking the location of the restless fish. Gillnets were, and still are, consistent killers of seabass.

Over two million pounds were landed annually from 1919 to 1922 and it was more than the resource could sustain. That catch rate has never been equalled and there has been a steady decline since. Imposition of closed seasons and size and possession limits in the 1930s proved to be too little too late. The fishery has not recovered to this day.

White seabass were still fairly abundant in the years before WW II, but the commercial catch dropped to 263,000 pounds in 1937. Dock totals of over 500 fish a day were sometimes recorded for the small San Diego sportboat fleet. For example: a single boat catch from the Coronados of 285 fish of not less than 25 pounds each was made on one 1935 trip and a record haul of 379 white seabass by 19 anglers was made at Catalina on September 11, 1938.

Although the largest commercial hauls of seabass were in nets, considerable numbers were taken by hook and line. Tons were caught at the Coronado Islands by San Diego market boats using handlines and live sardine baits. Further north they were mostly taken incidentally to barracuda and kelp bass fishing. Trolling sometimes produced fairly well and I dredged up a good many by that method in my commercial days. Large bone and aluminum jigs did the job. In the early 1970s seabass were caught commercially by poachers fishing under the schools of squid that assembled to spawn on the flats inshore of the Coronado Islands. A dozen or more plastic jugs were rigged with lengths of monofilament line secured to metal jigs. The jugs were put overboard where feeding birds indicated presence of squid. When a jug began to move and bob erratically it signalled that a white had seized the attached jig. A watchful fisherman would maneuver his boat, usually an outboard skiff, to pick up the jug and retrieve the fish. After a few seasons this small fishery, akin to jugging for catfish in freshwater, was halted by a shortage of squid and seabass and the increased vigilance of the Mexicans.

H & M charter boat with a dandy seabass haul.

Before the 1950s live squid were seldom available and the preferred bait was a live sardine or mackerel. In the days of hand-pulled cotton bait nets the seiners avoided setting on squid. Someone discovered how to catch the squirts with a light and a dip net or snag line and the candy bait has been the prime lure for white seabass ever since.

A suicidal unwariness seems to overtake seabass when they are hungry. They are not at all hook-shy—remember how many are taken on rent rods with the crudest of terminal tackle. The elimination of inshore gillnets and the promising hatchery program offer some hope that the noble croakers will again be a frequent part of anglers' future catches.

OCEAN HIPPOS

Relatively few sportfishermen today have ever seen a giant black sea bass, let alone caught one, so it is difficult to realize how abundant they once were and

Trolling with a Wilson spoon near Avalon was the method for taking this fish by the author.

how frequently they were captured. The big bass used to range along the whole South Coast and hundreds were taken by rod and reel from piers and barges. One of the largest on record was a seven-footer, weighing 539 pounds, that was found beached at San Clemente. This monster was about 60 years old. During the 1940s the fish were the target of intensive market fishing, particularly in Baja waters. The giant bass were hauled in on heavy handlines baited with chunks of sierra, barracuda or whitefish. When one came belly up to the gaff, it looked like "a hippopotamus without legs," as one fisherman put it. The last one I caught was on the Tanner Bank in 1973, a youngster of 66 pounds that ate the jig I was yo-yoing for salmon groupers.

Hollywood's Marty Buryan, veteran of 65 years of ocean fishing, was kind enough to share his experience on barges. Over the years he fished from many of the old hulks, concentrating on black sea bass, or jewfish as they were usually called. He tells of great catches long ago at Point Mugu and of the three bass he took from the barge MINNIE A. CAINE, and of the two big fish that famous reelmaker Arthur Kovalovsky landed from the pier at Hueneme.

Marty writes: "One Sunday while I was fishing for blacks from the barge VIRGINIA [at Malibu] a young lad came aboard and joined our crowd. Two weeks prior I had been fishing for black sea bass with regulation Tuna Club light tackle when a 50-pound halibut inhaled my mackerel bait. The boy had heard about it and inquired what his chances were for a big flattie. He was handed a tomcod which he impaled on his hook and cast overboard. His tackle consisted of a 12-foot Calcutta rod and a knuckle-buster reel with 200 yards of 27-pound test (nine thread) linen line. After pondering the situation I told our group that in spite of all the big game gear adorning the jewfish bridge it wouldn't be surprising if it was the lad that got a pick up. Believe it or not, about 15 minutes later his line took off with a black sea bass on one end and the boy with bruised knuckles on the other yelling, 'What shall I do?' I told him to hang on and pray! The worst thing was the reel wouldn't stay in gear. He appealed to me to take over and try to break the fish off to save the line. I told the gang to raise the skull and crossbones flag to summon the shoreboat MARINE GARDEN for assistance if the fish didn't spool me beforehand. When the boat came alongside I jumped to the foredeck. The skipper, Bob, asked what I had hooked up. When I said, 'Jewfish,' he retorted, 'Not on that outfit!' Off to sea we went, chasing the fish and one hour and twenty minutes later I brought a 190 pound black sea bass to gaff. After the deckhand and I pulled the fish aboard a nearby Fish & Game patrol boat came alongside and the warden couldn't believe the contraption I caught it with and said it should be a world record. In spite of the long rod and malfunctioning reel, it was fun while it lasted."

The L. A. Tribune reported in July 1929 that "Jewfish are so numerous at Santa Monica that recently, while a passenger on the boat COLLEEN was bringing in a halibut a large jewfish, estimated at 450 pounds, came to the surface and proceeded to devour the [halibut] bait, according to R. J. F. Oefinger of the Santa Monica Pleasure Fishing Boats. Capt. Chet Hedland of the COLLEEN gaffed the big fish who promptly started for the bottom, almost taking the captain with him. During the past week three black sea bass have been landed, Oefinger stated, and general fishing is splendid." In June, Oefinger himself took a 520-pounder and a month later caught a 256 pound bass in 14 minutes on 18 thread line. The huge fish was displayed and sold at the local Piggly Wiggly Market.

Big white seabass is a load for this youngster on barge POINT LOMA.

This noble croaker is one of many caught on barge POINT LOMA in 1928.

Happy farmers heft an ocean hippo.

Thirteen "Catalina Salmon" and a few yellowtail.

Chasing down a black seabass with a skiff near the Rock Pile below the Coronado Islands.

Barge VIRGINIA at Malibu.

Newport anglers found schools of seabass in the kelp beds below Dana Point.

Catching more than one giant bass in a day was commonplace in the first years of the century.

Fred Schipper lifts a Coronado Islands bass on boat SAN ANTONIO. Note hand-operated bilge pump in foreground, standard equipment on pre-WW II boats.

Earl Woods and friend show off Catalina rock cod, 1936.

"The Rock Codder," from a painting by the author.

Chapter 8
BOTTOM BANDITS AND FLUKES

"FLUKES!"

An incredible swarm of flatfish invaded Santa Monica Bay in the winter of 1933-34. The area has always been good for halibut, but old timers could not recall anything like it. They believed the fish were driven southward by a series of great storms in the northern waters of the state. Who knows? They may have been right.

In any case, the fishing was exceptional and at the peak of the run individual rod-and-reel catches of up to 30 fish in a day's drifting were common. In a couple of weeks the market price dropped from 10 cents a pound to three. Many of the fish kept would be "shorts" today, but about half were "counters" four pounds and above. I remember watching a commercial setline fisherman, knee-deep in halibut, in a skiff anchored near the pier. He spent a long afternoon filleting shorts to make them saleable. It may have been cheating, but a large percentage of setline fish were gut hooked and fishermen in those Depression days did not cut their leaders to release fish.

Much sportboat fishing was done within a few minutes run from the pier at spots then known as Marion Davies, Long Wharf, 101, and Big Rock. After some unproductive drifting, we would occasionally hit a concentrated pocket of halibut. Every rod on the lee side of the boat would bend at the same time, followed minutes later by hookups on the weather side. Crewmen scrambled frantically to answer cries for a gaff. During one fantastic drift I saw anglers bounce eight-pounders rather than wait for a busy gaffer.

The usual halibut rig was a two or three foot leader of gut or wire fastened by snap swivel to the bottom ring of a torpedo sinker. Hooks were usually 1/0 or 2/0 O'Shaughnessy, but a few anglers favored the Siwash pattern. Treble hooks were sometimes used, particularly if the bait was large. Theoretically the three-way hooks were less apt to foul the bait as the halibut mouthed it.

When the availability of horse sardine bait coincided with the presence of largish halibut the fishing could be very exciting. In clear water the active baits seemed to drive the flatfish berserk. Flying off the bottom, they would often

Old-timer displays barndoor halibut.

strike in a sizzling midwater run that would do credit to a yellowtail. We missed a few, but when we connected we could be sure of a good fish. Not many shorts were caught on big sardines.

Our slang name for halibut was "flukes" and the large ones were "army blankets" or "barndoors." The little guys were "postage stamps," and "flyswatters." Tourists from the East called them "flounders."

By concentrated effort during that memorable winter I learned the art of halibut fishing. It remains one of my favorite pastimes to this day. Coaxing halibut to bite can be challenging, but it is a restful, relaxed kind of fishing. It is still possible to catch more than a few flukes in a day's fishing, but I haven't landed over three keepers in one trip since the 22-inch size limit went into effect. Not long ago, while drifting San Diego Bay in a skiff, I reeled up 37 of the critters by actual count. Not one of them was of legal size. It

Sometimes a gentle nibbler.

was frustrating, but at least I know there are juveniles out there offering some promise for the future. I am also sure that we will never again see the likes of the great run of '34.

GOATS

Sheephead, whose Latin name *Pimelometopon pulchrum* means "beautiful fat forehead," were plentiful in Santa Monica Bay sixty years ago. Partyboats found them in kelp and reefs all the way to Pt. Dume and beyond. Armed with a purchase commitment from a customer, I would plan specifically for sheephead fishing. On the day before a trip fresh shelled mussels were prepared and live sandcrabs gathered. Using a handline baited with these tasty morsels it was not unusual to fill a sack with sheephead, along with other desirables such as cabezon, rockfish and huge perch. Hungry calico bass would also gulp a gob of mussel.

One memorable sheephead expedition took place in 1935. On a Friday afternoon, with a market order for "goats," my fishing buddy and I launched my 16-foot skiff through the surf. Rowing to the center of the pier, where mussels grew thick on the pilings, we pried off about 30 pounds of the shellfish. Next morning we were waiting a quarter mile north of the pier where we had a prearranged rendezvous with the all-day boat SCANDIA II. Skipper Joe Fudge had kindly agreed to take us in tow on his way to the Oil Well Spot off Zuma Beach, a famous hole for bull bass. With Joe's promise to pick us up on his way back, the skiff was cast off abreast of the headland.

A gigantic shark appeared...

Shipping the oars, we rowed quietly toward the great Seal Rock that lies off the tip of Pt. Dume. Because of a dangerous surge sportboats rarely fished there. Luckily, a calm sea enabled us to anchor about 50 feet from the white water boiling around the rocks. Here was rumored to be the lair of giant sheephead. To get their attention, I stomped a few pounds of mussels with booted feet and tossed the oozing shells overside. The chum soon took effect. Within minutes a huge pink spot grew in the clear water as hordes of sheephead massed under the skiff.

Attached to each heavy handline we had a sinker, wire leader and 2/0 hook. A juicy hunk of mussel for bait produced an instant bite. The strike was often felt as a gentle, perch-like nibble, but hookset could result in a sizzling, finger-burning run by a vigorous bull sheephead. We horsed them up hand over hand and in short order the bottom of the

Like sitting on a cactus.

skiff was covered with chunky red and black critters, one weighing over 25 pounds.

We enjoyed this wide open fishing for about an hour when, as if a switch was thrown, the bite suddenly ceased. In less than a second the red spot of schooled fish vanished. We remained puzzled for only a moment. Longer than the skiff, a gigantic shark appeared under the boat and then surfaced alongside. With dorsal fin towering over two feet above the water, the huge fish slowly circled. All at once we were feeling extremely vulnerable. When the thing finally swam off we quickly pulled anchor and rowed top speed into the center of the Dume kelp bed. There we languished until we met our towboat.

The shark incident is what makes this occasion so vivid in my memory. I had never seen one at that time, but I think now it was a harmless basking shark that we encountered. I seldom target sheephead these days, but each one caught reminds me of the startling appearance of the monstrous shark.

SCULPIN STORY

A rather mundane, unglamorous critter, the sculpin has always been in demand by discriminating sea food connoisseurs. They are a desirable commercial catch to this day, even though a labor intensive hook and line method is the only method to take them. In my commercial setline days I handled hundreds but was seldom stung by their poisonous fins. By keeping a firm grip on their lower jaws, I rarely needed pliers to remove the hooks.

The thorny sculpin.

My worst experience with sculpin occurred while market fishing. With two lines rigged with two hooks each, I was handlining them from my anchored boat. Spawning fish were thickly clustered over a spot of bottom structure. Alternately pulling, removing the fish, and rebaiting, I pulled sculpin aboard in a steady stream. To preserve their color, they were bounced directly into a fish box half full of crushed ice. Due to their relatively small size it took a great many fish to make a payday. They were good for gas and coffee money when nothing more lucrative was available.

The fish bit well and the box was filling up nicely. Up from the depths came another plump sculpin, a giant of its kind. Flopping as I swung it over the rail, it came unhooked and dropped, fins extended, onto my foot. A long dorsal spine penetrated the rubber boot and thick sock, stabbing deeply into my right big toe. The pain was instant and excruciating. After pulling off the boot I staggered to the cabin and lay rolling in agony, all thoughts of further fishing forgotten. After a couple of hours the pain subsided slightly and I was able to haul the anchor and get underway for port. It was well I had removed the boot as my injured foot was swollen to football size. Driving home was another ordeal and it was three days before I felt up to fishing again.

Commercial rock-codding.

Another horrendous happening occurred when an obnoxiously drunken sportboat passenger lurched with the roll of the boat and fell hard on a bulging gunny sack of sculpin. It must have been like sitting on a cactus or a huge pincushion. Aghast bystanders pulled the victim to his unsteady feet, but he seemed to feel little pain. Numerous blood spots on the seat of his pants testified, however, that he had been well and truly pierced. Perhaps his overload of booze temporarily anesthetized him, but I dare say he suffered a sort of double hangover the next day, hurting at both ends!

SCRUBS AND SLIMEYS

Traditionally, winter was the time South Coast fishermen put away their surface fishing gear and turned to probing the deep ocean for rock cod, more properly known as rockfish. Rock codding in the early days of sportfishing was a haphazard, hit or miss proposition at best. Many rockfish banks are too far offshore to be located with land-

Handlining rock cod on the SAN ANTONIO, 1933.

marks, especially on hazy or foggy days. Without the help of depth recorders, sonar or loran, captains relied on a compass course and specified running time to put them over a bank. When an area was reached, the boat began drifting. A buoy was put over to mark a spot of biting fish and subsequent drifts were made around the buoy.

Sport boats often had their bait tanks removed for winter fishing. Salted bait was deemed sufficient to lure unsophisticated rockfish and was provided in tubs placed about the deck. For fresher bait, mackerel and small fish caught during the trip were chunked.

The tackle employed was distinctly different than that used today. A few anglers converted their black seabass and marlin rigs, but most rock-codders used handlines of heavy cotton seine twine. Several boats specializing in winter fishing furnished free handlines wound on sticks. Also available as rental gear were large wooden reels that could be clamped to the boat's caprail. These winch-like contraptions were a foot or more in diameter and had a single action crank on the axle. They served mainly as a handy way to store the line as it was retrieved. Some dedicated fishermen built their own reels with a crank on each side so that both arms could share the arduous winding. The "stick-winders" coiled their lines on deck as they were pulled, hand-over-hand, but tangles were frequent. Whatever the method, rod and reel, winch or handline, rock codding was work.

Terminal tackle consisted of a number of 6\0 Kirby hooks, usually eight on rent gear, attached to the main line by short gangions of lighter cord. Commercial rockfish lines were called "feelers" and were essentially the same except that many more hooks per line, from forty to a hundred, were employed. To keep the thick lines on the bottom in deep water and strong currents, heavy weights were needed. Sinkers were cast iron window sash weights of two to eight pounds. No longer manufactured, sash weights are now rarely found. Lengths of steel rebar now serve the purpose on commercial lines.

During a fast drift in deep water it was nearly impossible to feel the fish biting. There was so much stretch in the cotton line that faint nibbles only were felt and the results would be in doubt until the retrieve. It was a good sign if the line commenced to go slack about half way up. It meant you had enough fish hooked to float the weight as decreasing pressure expanded their swim bladders.

My first rock cod trip in 1933 was to the South Bank in Santa Monica Bay. Fishing was poor and I had only a few small fish. When sold my catch would not suffice to repay my fare. Dejectedly, I dropped my handline for the last drift. No bites were felt, but when I hauled in the hooks held three large bocaccio that had inhaled mackerel snagged on the sink. My day was made!

Handlines for sportfishing were phased out in the 1950s as wire lines became standard for rod and reel. Flexible .024 Monel wire was usually wound on narrow spool Penn 49m reels mounted on fiberglass rods equipped with roller guides. Wire's inherent weight, minimal water resistance and lack of stretch made it possible to use much lighter sinkers to reach deep bottoms. The wiggle of a live anchovy 600 feet down can be felt with wire line, and the rattle of striking rockfish can be a real arm jerker.

Wire line has its drawbacks. Great care is required to prevent overruns on the drop. The wire's own weight builds momentum as it pays out and it will fall in coils if the sinker has already hit bottom. Kinks and breaks can result when the coils are rewound. Today, low-stretch synthetic Dacron has replaced wire lines.

Sixty years ago scrubs, boscos, Santa Marias and popbellies were our names for small rockfish such as starrys, greenspots, etc. Vermillion rockfish were redsnappers and

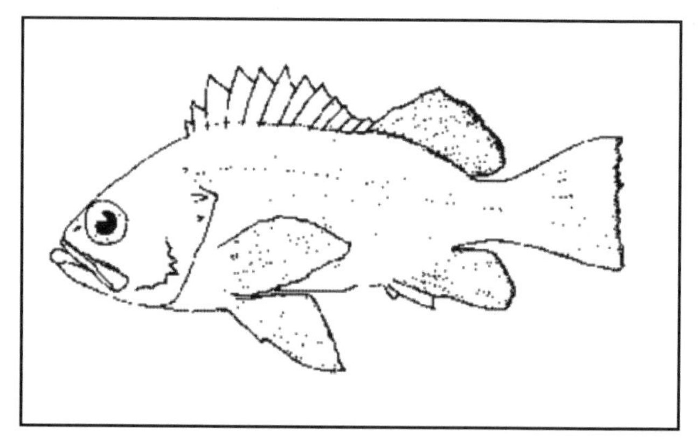

Vermillion rockfish, sometimes known as redsnapper.

Distracting a dangerous white-tip shark.

bocaccio were salmon groupers or slimeys. Widow rockfish were belinda cod but names such as barber pole, chucklehead and chili pepper applied to the same species as today.

SHARK ENCOUNTERS

How could those small fish pull that hard?" The thought flashed as I felt a strong tug on the rope stringer floating out behind me. A surge of adrenaline and a moment of panic came as I turned to find a large shark chomping a fish it had bitten from the stringer. Sixty feet of water separated me from the shore, most of it over my head, and the beast was between me and safety. It was hip deep where I stood atop my fishing platform, a coral mushroom jutting up from the lagoon bottom. The situation called for some immediate defensive action.

Quickly untying the stringer from my belt, I fastened it to the tip of my rod. A dangerous white-tip eight or nine feet long, the shark was only slightly distracted by its mouthful and was now obviously aroused and eager for more.

Were other predators also gathering? Sunset, when sharks came into the shallows to feed, was near. The low sun was at the wrong angle for me to see into the normally clear water. I dangled the remnants of my fish catch ahead of the shark's nose and it came, snapping. After leading it around to the open water side of the coral head, I hurriedly detached the stringer from my rod and tossed it some twenty feet out into the lagoon. The hungry shark responded as hoped and the second it charged the clump of fish I turned and struck out for the shore. Spurred by visions of gaping tooth-filled jaws at my heels, I swam at my best speed ever. Churning like an outboard motor, I hit the shallows. Scrambling shaken and breathless up the beach, I turned and saw the deadly fin still cutting the surface around the coral head.

The incident occurred at Eniwetok Atoll during my wartime duty there. I had fished from that coral head several times, wading and sidestroking out from the beach. The deep water on the offshore side was habitat for numerous small reef dwellers. It was the scent of fish blood in the water that drew the shark, and for that I had only myself to blame.

Later, fishing at night from a pier, I caught a number of large white-tips. Some unknown monster finally made off with the whole shark rig, popping the thick handline like a thread.

Another close encounter of the shark kind occurred a few years earlier near Newport Beach. After a successful day of barracuda jigging, I was gutting fish as my boat drifted a mile or so outside the jetties. Standing in the steering cockpit in the stern I was close to the water and, by leaning over slightly, able to hold the dressed fish by the gills and slosh them up and down for rinsing. Nearing the end of my chore, I grew somewhat absentminded. While gazing at the horizon I anticipated an evening's entertainment. My fish earnings would afford a visit to the Balboa ballroom to hear Stan Kenton's orchestra.

As I sloshed a barracuda there came a fierce jerk and sound of snapping. Hastily withdrawing my arm I held up a head, cleanly severed. The fish's body had disappeared into the maw of a ten-foot hammerhead shark! It had missed seizing my hand by inches. After scarfing up the guts that had chummed it to the boat, the shark had tried for a bigger bite. Ghastly visions of a torn and bleeding stump filled my head as I started the engine. After moving the boat some distance the cleaning task had my undivided attention until completed.

Famous Catalina guide Mexican Joe and young angler pose with an impressive hammerhead shark, c. 1902.

Catching three-pole tuna, a strenuous and exciting method not much used today.

The author once owned this ancient double-ended troller. Note steadying sail on forestay and mackerel-scooping rack on stern.

Part IV
FISHING FOR MONEY
Chapter 9
FORGOTTEN TECHNIQUES

Several methods of small scale commercial fishing are described here. Some of the techniques constitute a lost art and it is unlikely that any of them will ever again be employed. On the other hand, if near shore gillnetting is eliminated and market demand is sufficient, there may come a day when a hook-and-line commercial fisherman may once again gather a modest living from the sea. Until about 1950, barracuda and white seabass were abundant enough to support a troll fishery for the fresh market. When albacore were not available hundreds of small one-man boats worked the waters between Santa Monica and San Diego in pursuit of these species. Trolling was a seasonal activity usually carried on in spring and early summer. When not dragging jigs, many boats switched to scooping mackerel or setlining for bottomfish. In northern waters somewhat different techniques were used, but salmon trolling remains a viable pursuit to this day.

BARRACUDA METHODOLOGY

A long bronze shape suddenly materialized out of the blue-green depths and the dipping, wavering of the lure disappeared. A quick upward heave on the long bamboo pole and another six-pound barracuda thumped into the fish bin. Writhing and flopping, the fish spit the barbless hook and the lure was returned to the water ready for the next strike. The action was repeated again and again as the pile of fish grew. As many as 80 barracuda could fill the bins at the end of a good day. It was a productive way of market fishing during the 1930s.

The method, known as "wiggle-poling" and akin to "squidding" for tuna, was only one of the techniques used by small-boat commercial fishermen. It was most deadly when the fish were concentrated in a chum line or on "meat balls" of anchovies. Sportfishing boats were often sur-

Wiggle-poling barracuda.

rounded by small commercial craft taking advantage of the chumming.

The basic equipment for wiggle-poling was simple and inexpensive, an important consideration for marginal operators in those economic hard times. A stout cane pole about 16 feet long, a short piece of strong cotton line, a swivel, two eight-foot lengths of #8 and #6 gauge blued stainless wire, and a specially hand-tied lure made up the gear.

For barracuda fishing, a skipjack-size Japanese tuna squid was stripped of its short feathers and retied with eight or ten long (4 inch) white plumes with perhaps a couple in blue or red. These were secured to the hook shank with many tight turns of light brass or copper wire. Streamlining and extra protection for the feathers was provided by layers of white adhesive tape or a skin mantle over the wire.

With its weighted head, single barbless hook and trailing tail of undulating feathers, the lure was as deadly a killer of ocean fish in its time as the plastic grubs are today. Not only barries, but all surface species, including white seabass and calicos, were eager for it. Even halibut and yellowfin croaker struck when it came into their deeper habitat, and it was effective for largemouth bass in fresh water.

Called simply a "barracuda feather" or "barracuda striker" it was employed in a variety of ways. A variation of wiggle-poling was "poke-poling," a type of slow trolling wherein the boat proceeded at idling speed as the pole and lure were trailed in the water astern. To impart a darting action to the feather the fisherman held the butt of the pole and swung his arm in a poking motion. When a strike was felt both hands were, of course, used to lift the fish aboard. It was not uncommon for the pole to be snatched clean away when hit by the odd heavy fish, white seabass or yellowtail being the usual culprits. Some fishermen secured a loose safety line to the butts of two poles and poked with both arms while moving the boat tiller with feet or legs. When a pole was hit the other would be dropped and allowed to trail by its safety line while the fish was boated. The action could be hot and heavy when double hookups occurred.

When barracuda were scattered or holding deep, a method known as "jerk-lining" was employed. A handline eight or ten fathoms in length was rigged with a length of #6 wire leader and weights up to two pounds. Proceeding at a slow troll, the fisherman held the line and swung his arm in rhythmic strokes until the strike. The fish was then rapidly pulled in, hand over hand.

The feather was also fished with great success on rod and reel. For casting weight a plated torpedo sinker with a trailing 3-foot leader was rigged. The lure was cast as far as possible and retrieved with a fast start and stop action to impart a darting motion to the feather. Anglers partial to the technique were known as "feather merchants."

Trolling bone and aluminum jigs on multiple long lines spread by outriggers was the more traditional method of taking barracuda. In Santa Monica Bay one of the most productive sectors for jigging was from El Segundo to Venice. The Marina Del Rey tract was a sparsely settled expanse of truck farms bisected by Ballona Creek, a flood drainage channel.

The area's greatest fish attractor was the Hyperion sewer outfall, where all Los Angeles dumped its waste. It welled up to the surface in a huge boil of thick brownish water dotted with bits of indescribable flotsam. Depending on current flow, the discolored water often spread north to Venice and south to Hermosa. Sometimes it lay on the sur-

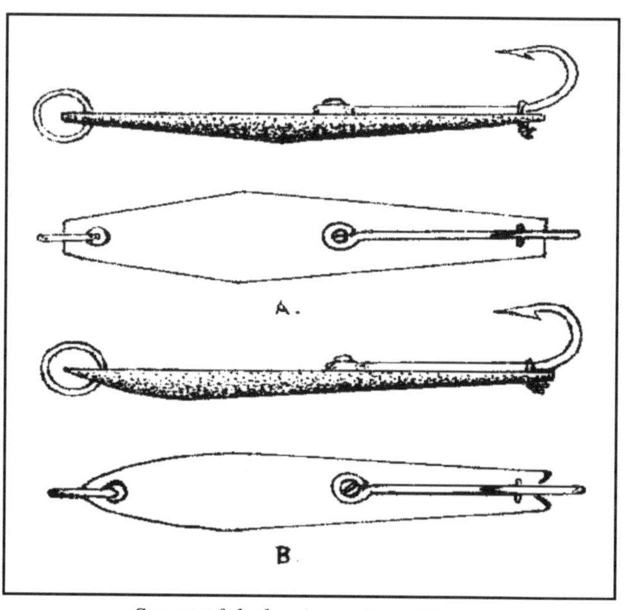

Successful aluminum jig patterns.

face as a film only a foot or two in depth with the clean water underneath. At any rate, the sewer bubble was alive with thousands of scavenging smelt. These in turn attracted large numbers of barracuda and white seabass. In my commercial days I took hundreds of those two species and a goodly number of kelp bass and halibut from the brown water. Over the years, tons of fish were taken in the vicinity, but I never heard anyone complain that the contaminated sea might poison the catch. Apparently, the theory was that if the fish could survive in it unharmed they would be fit to eat.

Keeping an eye peeled for working birds, I would troll a zigzag course that would eventually bring me to the sewer bubble, which always got a good working over. Many good-sized seabass came right from the middle of the beige water column. The other best area seemed to be off the Ballona jetties and a mile or two either side, fairly close to shore. When it was shallow enough that the weights would bounce the bottom, I could expect strikes from halibut. A twenty-pounder on the end of the jig line put up a pretty violent resistance, let me tell you. It was likely that they would tear loose if horsed in the same manner as albacore.

The rubber shock cords only twitched a bit when barries bit, but were well-stretched when heavier fish hit. It was easy to tell when seabass or halibut were on the line by the head-shaking fight they made as I drew them in, hand over hand.

There must have been a slight flavor of fresh water, however polluted, in the area that attracted the 17-pound salmon and the beautiful eight-pound steelhead I took off Ballona Creek. Both struck a white bone jig. The sea-run rainbow trout, poor lost creature, was evidently looking for a spawning stream as she spewed bright red eggs when dropped in the fish box.

Since moving to San Diego forty years ago I haven't fished in Santa Monica Bay so can't comment on the current productivity of the waters there, but it may be of interest to know that the vicinity of the marina was once a prime fishing spot.

The illustration below shows a successful rig for commercial barracuda and seabass trolling. There were some minor variations according to the personal whims of individual fishermen. Monofilament line would probably be incorporated in some parts of a modern array and the single fixed-hook metal jigs popular for sportfishing would no doubt be equally effective for commercial trolling.

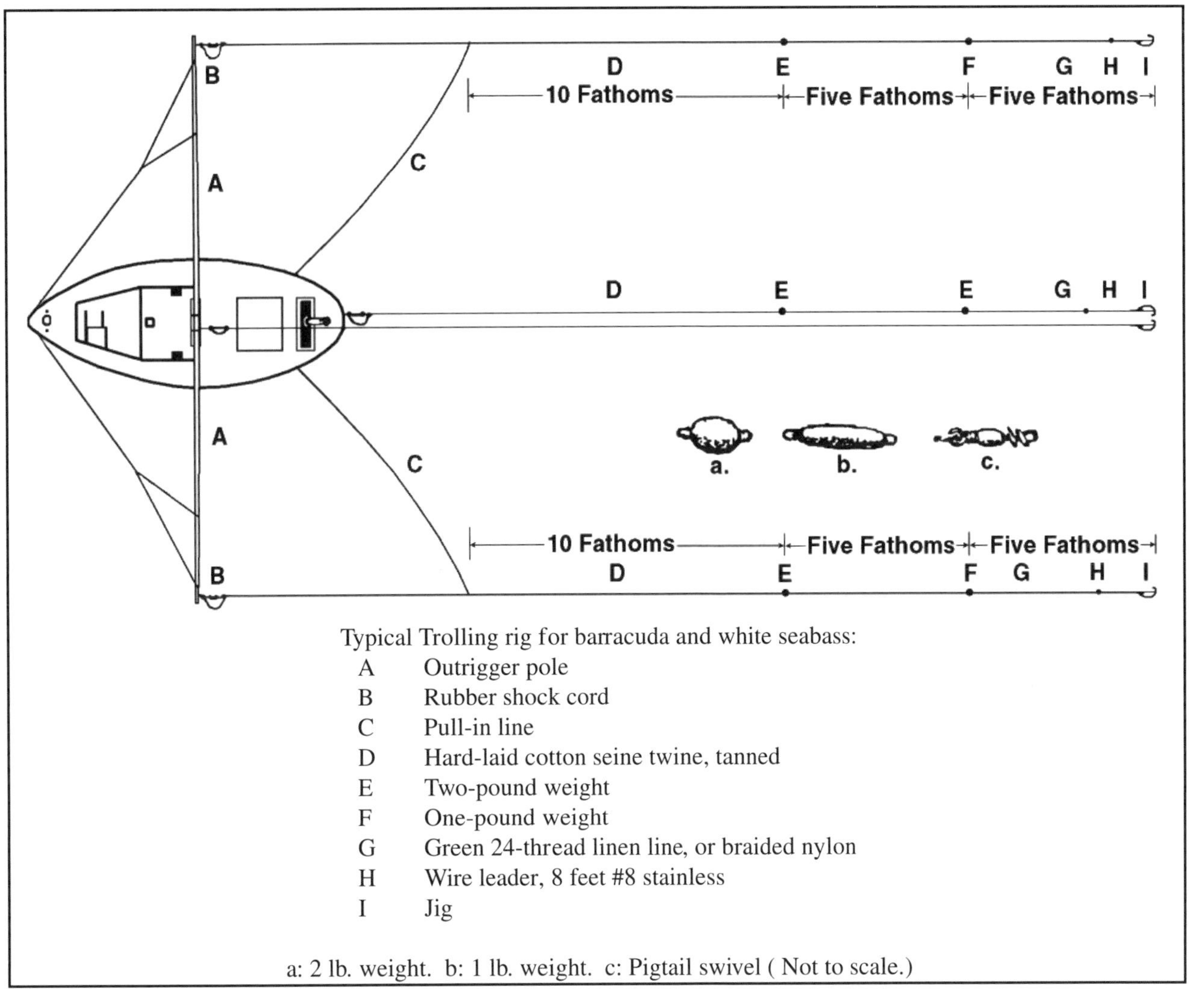

Typical Trolling rig for barracuda and white seabass:

A Outrigger pole
B Rubber shock cord
C Pull-in line
D Hard-laid cotton seine twine, tanned
E Two-pound weight
F One-pound weight
G Green 24-thread linen line, or braided nylon
H Wire leader, 8 feet #8 stainless
I Jig

a: 2 lb. weight. b: 1 lb. weight. c: Pigtail swivel (Not to scale.)

The author boats another trolled barracuda. Note bone jig and weights on caprail.

Runs of large bonito seem to occur only sporadically, but I recall one memorable year when I fished them commercially for a small local cannery. In the fall of 1966 swarms of big bonito and yellowtail were present off San Diego from Point Loma to La Jolla. Trolling from the Whistler Buoy northward I found them schooling from two to four miles offshore. Apparently unaware of the concentrations of fish outside, the half-day boats were content picking bass and a few yellows in the kelp.

Dragging bone and aluminum jigs on five-fathom lines, I pulled hundreds of bonito and yellowtail amounting to nearly five tons in 15 days of fishing. The bonito averaged 7 1/2 pounds in weight and the yellows averaged 15. My best daily score, on October 9th, was 147 bonito and 52 yellowtail for 1,796 pounds. I haven't found fishing like that so close to home since. Mine was the only jig boat working the area then and I haven't seen a commercial troller fishing inshore since. The large fish don't seem to assemble in such numbers these days, although the half-day boats occasionally find fair fishing on jig strikes.

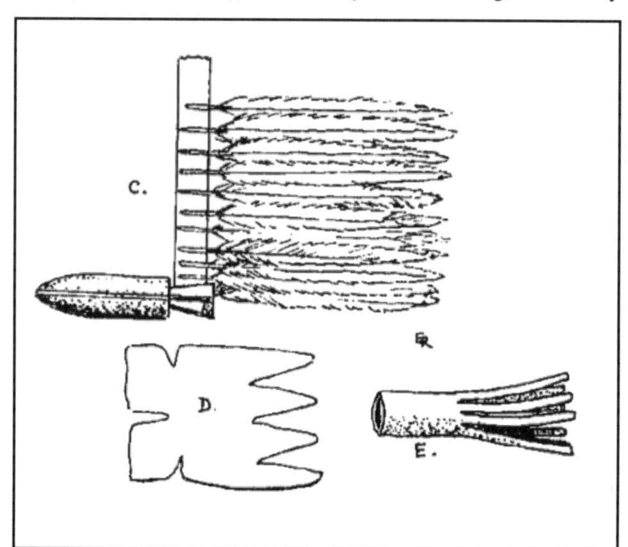

Method for overhauling feather jigs.

MAKING JIGS IN THE OLD DAYS

Japanese bone jigs were the favored lure of trollers, but they were often altered to provide a more seductive wobble at slow barracuda trolling speed, about half of albacore jig speed. This was usually done by filing down the hump on the bottom of the jig and sharpening the nose somewhat, thus reducing the amount of spin and providing more side to side action. It was a matter of trial and error and when a successful fish-catching design was achieved the pattern was closely guarded. The war cut off supplies of Japanese tackle so attempts were soon made to duplicate productive designs in pot metal and plastic. The famous plastic Baldy's were produced in Newport Beach, homeport of a large jigboat fleet, and some of them were very good indeed.

A number of fishermen made their own lures from aluminum flat bar, 5 or 6 inches long and about 1¼ inches greatest width. The outline was cut from the bar with a hacksaw and then the bottom or hump side was shaped by filing. The finished product was polished and protected by clear lacquer, or sometimes painted white. With all the time and tedious hand labor involved it became a real disaster when a jig was lost. The Starman "Candy Bar" jigs are very similar, and may have been derived from the handmade patterns.

It was about this time that plastic heads for feather jigs made their appearance. They all had a plain bullet shape and came in a variety of semitransparent colors. Many fishermen tied up their own jigs using the heads and bundles of feathers purchased at commercial tackle shops.

My method was to cut a piece of scotch tape about eight inches long and turn both ends under, sticking them to a table top. This left about six inches of the sticky side facing up. Feathers were then selected and the short fuzz at the quill end stripped off. Next the quills were pressed to the tape at close intervals until there was enough to make a nice, fluffy jig. The tails of the feathers were laid on uniformly as the natural taper in each would fair out the tail of the completed jig. The excess of quills was trimmed to the edge of the tape with small scissors. The tape with attached feathers was then carefully lifted, the end stuck to the jig head and the whole wrapped tightly.

The completed wrap was further secured by a few turns of fine brass wire and then covered by a protective skirt of skin or plastic for which I had made a paper pattern. Dried dorado or halibut skin was excellent for this purpose as it was tough and also very pliable when wet. Plastic surgical tubing was also used for skirts and I found scraps of synthetic canvas from sailmakers to be useful. I tried it on my albacore "squids," or strikers, and even when the feathers had been chewed off the fish would still hit the rugged white material.

Plastic strands of lawn chair webbing can be substituted for feathers or combined with them. It was interesting to try various color combinations and I continued to tie my own jigs every year up until I ceased to fish commercially. Today's fancy factory-made jigs with their beautiful eyeballs, etc. are very efficient fish attractors. Unless he is an inveterate tackle tinkerer, the sportfisherman today has no reason to make his own.

The setliner.

THE SET LINER

When surface fish were unavailable the small, one-man trollers turned to bottom fishing. The gear used by nearly all these little vessels was the longline, dressed with hundreds of hooks, each one on a short leader. The rig was most often deployed as an anchored setline for bottom fish and occasionally as a midwater drift line for mackerel. The method is ancient and labor intensive, with few changes over the centuries. Now automation and hi-tech equipment have generated renewed interest in the old technique.

For setlining and general purpose fishing, I began with a leaky 16-foot skiff purchased in 1936. To construct my array, I bought a 2 1/2 pound hank of 72 thread cotton seine twine. It was dyed a rich brown color by preservative tanning. No. 15 line was used to make 18-inch leaders for 300 6/0 Kirby hooks. Clove hitches secured the leaders to the ground line at four foot intervals. Each end of the 1,250 foot main line was anchored by a five-pound sash weight attached to a buoy line. The whole rig was carefully coiled into a shallow tub. Better-equipped professionals stored lines on specially made flat wicker baskets, securing hooks in strips of cork fitted around the rims.

Bait was salted down from a previous trip or preferably procured fresh from one of the bait haulers or passenger boats. In Santa Monica I was acquainted with all the crews and usually had no difficulty bumming a couple of scoops. That was enough for one day as the scoops then were large containers, not the small tennis racket affairs used today.

After obtaining bait I had to row to a fishing area, or arrange a tow by one of the sport boats. Fortunately, good halibut grounds were close by and I thought nothing then of rowing a mile or two in the morning calm. Fishing was mostly northwest of the pier where the usual afternoon wind and chop gave a homeward push. An outboard motor was soon acquired for the skiff and later setlining was from a series of power boats.

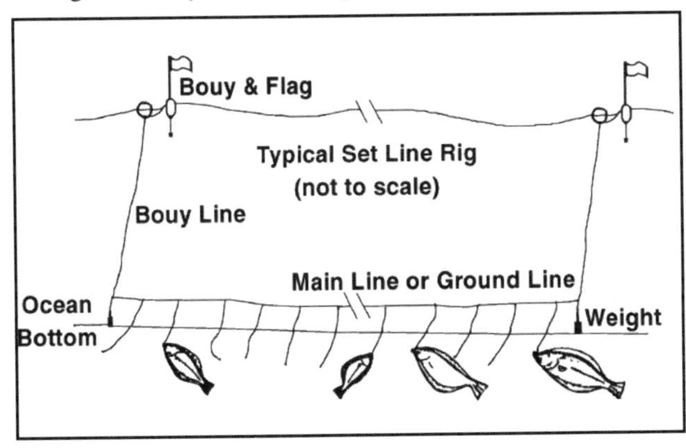

Typical set line rig.

Once at the chosen spot the first weight was dropped and line was paid out as the skiff drifted with the current or was helped along with the oars. Each hook was baited with a rapidity that increased with practice. When the set was complete, it was back to the first buoy to lift the line. The weight was returned to the water, but the main line was retained and under-run. Fish were removed and hooks rebaited as the skiff was pulled along the line. Current and drift drug the line somewhat during each run, thus covering unfished areas of the bottom. It took a little over an hour to run the line. If I got an early start I could make the set and four or five under-runs, thus presenting 1500 to 1800 baits.

Halibut were the main target, but sand bass, sculpin and rockfish filled out the catch. Tomcod (white croaker) were the most numerous catch and mackerel were sometimes a plague. All sorts of sharks, skates and rays gulped the baits and large ones caused some nasty tangles when they rolled in the line. Soupfin, leopard sharks and skates were marketable, but the rest were just varmints. Midshipmen and ratfish were a nuisance as were slime eels, or hagfish. The obnoxious creatures would eat their way inside a hooked halibut and leave only a bag of skin and bones. Once in a great while a serendipity of white seabass would occur and I once took a black seabass of 120 pounds on my set line. It was exhausting work but it was another way to make a scarce Depression dollar.

SCOOPING MACKEREL

Pacific mackerel were once the basis of a thriving industry that furnished employment for hundreds of fishermen and cannery workers. The bulk of the product for human consumption was exported to the Orient. Before 1950 mackerel fishing was not confined to seiners alone, but supported a large fleet of smaller boats using another method. Unbelievable as it may seem, tons of free-swimming mackerel were actually scooped from the ocean with hand-held dip nets.

Daylight mackerel fishing. Lad in foreground is using a striker pole.

Using the scoop method, introduced in 1933, one man could catch as much as three tons of greenbacks in a night's fishing and two men could boat six tons. The equipment needed was simple and specialized. A basic boat, a powerful spotlight, and a scoop net about two feet in diameter and 30 inches deep fitted to a stout five-foot handle, were minimum. A fishing rack made from steel reinforcing rods completed the equipment. When fishing, the cage-like rack

Free-swimming mackerel are scooped and flung aboard.

was hung over the port or starboard quarter so that a man standing in it had his feet at or near the waterline. A rail supporting him at waist level allowed free movement of body and arms. For chum, ground bait in 50-gallon drums was furnished by the cannery.

When the moon was dark, scoop boats would time their departure from port to arrive at the fishing area an hour before sunset. A gunny sack of chum was hung overboard where its juices could lay down a slick while drifting. If mackerel were in the area they would soon appear and were assessed as to their size and abundance. If the school was large and hungry the boat was anchored, the light was rigged and the rack positioned.

After donning boots and oilskins the crew was ready to fish. A bucket was filled with a soupy mixture of chum and water. The spotlight was aimed at the surface directly in front of the rack. When the fish were sufficiently concentrated the fisherman would climb into the rack. Holding the scoop in his left hand, with his right he would toss a fistful of soupy chum into the circle of light. A milky cloud

Unloading scooped mackerel at a Newport cannery. Rack is visible at lower left. Drums held chum.

would form into which the hungry mackerel would charge *en masse*. The scoop was lowered to a spot up current from the chum cloud and the frenzied frogs, blinded by hunger and the milky water, would rush headlong into the net. By simultaneously lifting and scooping a burden of live fish, as much as 50 pounds at a time, was trapped and flung into the boat over the fisherman's shoulder. The entire boat was soon covered by a continuous shower of blood, scales and bits of chum put up by the kicking mass of fish. The scooping would proceed until weary arms and backs forced a halt. Unless the mackerel were spooked by marauding sharks or sea lions, the fishing could continue until deck bins were full. At the cannery fish were unloaded on a first come-first served basis, but had to be delivered inside 12 hours to prevent spoilage. While waiting in line for access to the cannery pier there was time for a meal and a nap. Once alongside, more backbreaking labor with wire shovels transferred the fish to adjustable hoppers set at rail level, whence they travelled by conveyor belt into the cannery. It was often possible to hire odd-job workers to unload the catch. A fresh drum of chum was taken aboard and the crew was free to snatch a few hours rest before setting out for another night of fishing. From a low of $8 a ton in 1932 the price rose to $21 by 1937. A minor bonanza for the fishermen was possible as long as the mackerel were available within a reasonable distance of the cannery ports. Scooping as a method lasted about 20 years, but this interesting and unlikely form of fishing will probably never be seen again.

SAN QUINTIN ALBIES

My first view of Bahia San Quintin was from the seaward approach to the narrow channel winding into the lagoon. The date was July 27th, 1948. A small trolling boat had carried me there on a commercial albacore expedition. At the time it was isolated and little known to Yankees.

San Quintin has recently become the base for growing numbers of anglers intent on sampling the excellent fishing at nearby San Martin Island, Ben's Rock and offshore banks. The new fish camp at the Old Mill offers good accommodations for visiting fishermen. Yellowtail, white seabass and all varieties of kelp bed and bottom fish are to be had.

Few of today's visitors are aware of the much different events at San Quintin 50 years ago. An American cannery, intent on satisfying a huge postwar demand for canned tuna, established a buying barge to purchase albacore. An old ferry hulk was obtained somewhere and moored in the backwaters of the bay. Hundreds of trollers unloaded and weighed in their catches on the barge. Gasoline in drums was available for refueling and groceries were supplied in limited amounts at high cost. The fish were carried ashore in an LCVP war-surplus landing craft. Trucks hauled the albacore on their final journey to the cannery in San Diego and returned with groceries and drums of gas. For a couple of months the activity was intense.

Due to pilferage and decay of the fish during transport, the enterprise was not a success for the cannery. The buying station, however, enabled many small jig boats to participate in the hot albacore fishing outside San Martin. Most small trollers were unable to keep fish for more than a day without spoilage. Daily refueling was also necessary for many boats. Without the barge to take their catches and

The albacore buying barge at San Quintin, 1948.

My last troller. From the author's painting.

provide fuel they would have been confined to less-productive day trips from San Diego or other South Coast ports.

Albacore, in their erratic way, had reappeared in California waters during the 1940s. The really good fishing was along the barren Mexican coast outside the range of most small boats. During the first few years after the war the canneries set up, in addition to the San Quintin barge, buying stations at San Martin Island, Cape Colnett, Todos Santos, San Clemente and Catalina Islands.

Large numbers of small to medium sized trollers, known generically as "jig boats," were built or converted in the years immediately following World War II. It was a peculiar time in fishing history. Thousands of young veterans, many with wartime savings to spend, were looking for employment. Big bucks were being earned by albacore fishermen. The appeal of fishing for a living was irresistible. Besides, there were hundreds of war surplus water craft available for a song.

LCP and LCVP landing boats were favorites for conversion to fishing duties. The ramps were removed from LCVPs and keel extensions and stem pieces added. Bow sections were formed with marine plywood and the hulls were decked over to provide fish holds, etc.

The famous PT boats and other war craft had proved the value of plywood in small vessel construction. In addition to conversion work it was widely used for new hulls. Heavy old-style planked displacement designs were still favored for craft over 35 feet, but small plywood boats were cheap and quickly built. Light and fast, they were extremely popular for multipurpose fishing.

A friend bought one of the 26-foot models built at the Jeffries yard in Santa Monica. Powered by a Ford V-8 engine the boat was fast and agile. Two eucalyptus saplings served as outrigger poles to spread the trolling lines. As a fishing partner, I provided the knowhow and we began our albacore season operating from San Diego.

Competing canneries drove the price up to an unprecedented $640 a ton and even $720 for a brief time. Boats from as far as Alaska migrated south to participate in the bonanza. From midnight to dawn the dark ocean offshore

Another of the author's small commercial boats. Backyard-built boats of this type were known as "pots."

from San Diego sparkled with a great galaxy of running lights as the fleet sortied for the day's fishing. Each evening the swarm of returning boats formed a huge traffic jam around the cannery pier at Point Loma. Shelter Island did not yet exist and the sportboats still operated from the downtown embarcadero.

After two weeks at San Diego we obtained Mexican permits and topped off our fuel. Drawn by rumors of fabulous fishing to the south, we set out on the 153 mile passage. Averaging nine knots we made the run in 17 hours, arriving at San Quintin about 5 PM.

It was a somewhat daring journey for a 26-foot gas boat and with no radio and only a pair of lifejackets for safety equipment. We were not the only risk-takers. At least two sister boats and a couple of Jeffries 30-footers were also at San Quintin. On one occasion I informed a Mexican lad working on the barge that we needed "gasolina por el barco." His disdainful reply: "No es barco, es skeef!" We got no respect!

We worked as far as seventy miles offshore. Every night scores of boats passed near or over dangerous Ben's Rock on their way to sea, but I never heard of anyone bumping. Fishing was indeed better than off San Diego and we managed nearly six tons of albacore for ten days of trolling. When we later redeemed our fish tickets we received only 26 cents a pound instead of the 32 cents paid for deliveries at San Diego.

Our diet was less than healthy, consisting mostly of peanut butter and jelly sandwiches and canned stuff heated on a Coleman stove. Bottled soda was our drink. We slept on either side of the engine in the boat's tiny forward cabin. Washing was done with sea water.

Overcoming fatigue was (and is) the greatest challenge in albacore fishing. Our light craft bobbed over the waves like a cork and balancing against the constant motion hour after hour was exhausting. To avoid going overboard on one very rough trip we had to sink to our knees while pulling the 1,500 pounds of fish we caught.

The San Quintin buying station was replaced the following year by a refrigerated tuna transport ship anchored at San Martin. I fished a larger, more comfortable diesel-powered boat that year. My last visit to San Quintin bay was in 1950 when I steered another albacore chaser there in search of bait. We found it, too, making a good haul of mixed anchovies and sardines.

THREE POLE THRILLS

After a summer of albacore jig fishing along the upper Baja coast, I signed on for a bait boat trip in October of 1949. By that time the troll fishing in local waters had waned, but there were still some good catches to be made near Guadalupe Island. We were four in the crew, including the skipper-owner.

After making bait above Cape Colnett, we chugged straight out on the 135-mile run to the island. Nary a jig strike was had until we were some five miles from the isle. As we slid into the stop I noticed enormous boils in the chum line. "What huge albacore!" was my thought as I scrambled into the rack. With a tremendous jerk on the pole my squid lure was instantly nailed by a blackbacked torpedo. The line snapped and I flopped on my stern. It was soon apparent that a school of tuna had come to us and that they were big guys, a hundred pounds on up. We watched helpless and fascinated as the hungry giants foamed around the boat. Our single albacore poles could not handle the monsters and no multiple-pole sets were ready rigged.

The skipper, frustrated beyond endurance, rushed below to fetch a ball of heavy cotton handline. Armed with a wire leader and a 10/0 hook, it was part of the gear used in winter market fishing for black seabass and grouper along the Baja coast. Spearing a salted sardine on the hook he tossed it overboard, meanwhile searching for a handy object around which to take a turn of line.

Instantly seizing the bait, a huge tuna streaked off in an express-train run. The friction of dry twisted line zipping through unwary fingers caused some frantic fumbling and cussing as blisters rose. Unable to get a firm grip on the smoking twine, our leader flung the whole ball overboard and plunged his burning digits into the cooling bait water. The rest of the crew found the action hilarious.

Vowing not to be caught unprepared again, we left the school to a better equipped boat. A search of the tackle drawer produced the necessary heavy duty brass ring with

Larger albacore chaser. Note double bait tanks.

four swivels, a wire pigtail and an extra-large squid. Three of the spare bamboo poles were bridled to the ring with heavy line and the squid was hung to the pigtail. The rig was stored in a handy location under the bait tank canopy.

Our second chance came a couple mornings later. We got jig bit a scant quarter mile from the island and it was tuna on the hook. In the clear, calm water we could see huge dark barrel shapes darting through the wake. The time had come to break out our three-pole rig.

The next forty minutes marked one of the most memorable events in my fishing experience. It was incredibly wild, strenuous and exciting. Shooting straight up from the depths, a tuna would engulf the dangling squid. Heaving together, the three of us on the poles yanked their heads out of the water. Momentum from powerful thrashing tails helped carry them over the rail. As the heavy bodies slammed the deck the barbless hook flew free and was whipped back into the sea. The great crescent tails drummed the deck, showering us with blood and water. Panting and sweating with our exertions, we hollered at each strike. The fish seemed to get larger and we had difficulty with a couple we couldn't lift enough to clear the rail. When they finally left us we had captured nearly two tons of the critters. We believed them to be yellowfin but they probably were bigeyes. A distinction between the two was seldom made at the time.

We found no more schooled tuna on that trip but there were other interesting moments. Lone specimens often mixed with the albacore and I hauled in a sixty-pounder by backing my pole hand over hand and trussing the tuna's head to the rack rail until the chummer hopped down and gaffed it. There was no way one pole could lift a fish that size.

Only a very few bait boats remain in the commercial fishery, but before the advent of the giant seiners in the 1960s ninety percent of the canned product was taken on hook and line. Film of pole fishing for big tuna survives and some exciting footage has been transferred to video tape. It is readily available and no fisherman can view it and fail to be stirred by the wild action.

GUADALUPE TALES

Guadalupe Island's distance from coastal bait grounds behooved us to be conservative in our use of the live stuff. After expending half our anchovies we found a drifting kelp paddy several miles from the island. A school of small jack mackerel hovered under the fronds and the skipper decided to try a set with the bait net. A couple of large tiger sharks were also cruising in the vicinity.

After stacking the net we put the skiff over with a man to grapple the paddy and hold it in the center of the circled webbing. It was no easy task for three of us to haul the net from a drifting boat. To our dismay the jacks took alarm and came scooting out through the large mesh of the wings. After a few moments darting this way and that, the small macs apparently decided the sharks were a greater menace and swam back under the paddy where we soon sacked them up. Now ensued the really arduous part of the operation. Without losing the bait, the slimy wads of kelp had to be removed from the net by hand and dumped outside the corkline. We ended up with 30 scoops of three-inch stuff, hardy in the tank and on a hook. Tiny, brilliantly colored yellowtail and inch-long perfectly formed salmon groupers were mixed with the mackerel.

A drawback to the small jacks as bait was the line of bony scutes along their sides. The tiny thorns were very hard on water softened hands, particularly those of the chummer, and were also detrimental to the remaining 'chovies. When chumming we learned to toss them well away. Instinctively seeking shelter under the nearest floating object, they darted straight back to the boat.

Another crew, low on bait, learned of our successful paddy haul and tried the same ploy. Their set went awry and the boat drifted over the net, severely damaging it with the propeller. For room to stretch and patch, they took the net to the rocky beach of the north anchorage. It was nearly dark when repairs were finished. Intending to bring the net aboard next morning, they launched their skiff and returned to their vessel for the night. Imagine their chagrin when daylight disclosed only a plume of smoke and a few charred corks and leads where the net had been. Apparently set by a carelessly flung cigarette butt, a smoldering fire had completely destroyed the webbing. It was a very short payday for that hard luck crew at trip's end.

On a calm evening at the island anchorage a friend from a neighboring boat was paddling our way for a visit. A great white shark rose under his dinghy, a terrifying sight. To the shark the boat and splashing oars doubtless bore some resemblance to a swimming elephant seal. Short oars churned up a froth as the tall dorsal fin cut the surface behind the tiny craft. The frightened visitor leaped onto our boat and disappeared below while I retrieved his dropped oars and tied up the dinghy. Fascinated, I stared at the huge beast cruising slowly back and forth below our stern. Preceded by pilot fish, the predator was followed by a score of yellowtail, nudging and jostling, as is their way with sharks. Twice he rolled slightly to give me a chilling look with an opaque black eye. Our visitor did not return to his own vessel until the next morning.

Followed by a score of yellowtail.

Trollers and bait boats fish for albacore in the Catalina Channel, c. 1917. From a painting by the author.

Albacore boats wait to unload their cleaned and beheaded catch, 1911.

Chapter 10
THE CHICKEN OF THE SEA

The status of albacore changed from pest to valued prize when it was discovered that after canning they were similar in taste to chicken. The years 1903 to 1910 were developmental and the first large pack of 20,000 cases of canned albacore was made in 1911. From then on the white meat tuna was sought by an ever-growing fleet of commercial boats.

Albacore could not be caught in nets and the entire catch was taken by labor-intensive hook and line methods. In addition to large numbers of fishermen, several thousands of people from cannery workers to boatbuilders were employed as a result of the tuna fishery. It was a bonanza—an ocean gold rush.

In 1917 albacore were pursued by some 500 boats from San Pedro alone. Tuna Red, a special paint developed by a local ship chandler, was used to cover bait tanks and inboard surfaces of bulwarks and fish bins. Zane Grey wrote that on one day that year he counted 132 boats cruising the Catalina channel. "I have become used to seeing dots of red all over the ocean...They ran to and fro...chasing every white splash, and they make every angler's pleasure taste bitter."

In 1913 there were two small canneries operating in San Diego, packing 12,000 cases of albacore a year. They were supplied by about 15 boats fishing within 12 or so miles of Pt. Loma. To complete unloading before the working day ended for shore people, they had to return by 2 PM. Catches were limited by the canneries to 1,000 pounds daily per boat. Thirty dollars a ton cleaned, heads off, was paid to the fishermen for their efforts. With a half-ton limit, the maximum total earning per boat per day was $15. On a good day, after deducting expenses and owners shares, the crew might wind up with two dollars each. Dollars then were worth twenty-five times present value.

The fascinating photo above was taken in 1911. Waiting to unload, the afterdeck of each boat is filled to the rails with plump albacore, already gutted and beheaded. Standing deep in fish are the crew members, four on one boat and two on the other. These were probably handline boats since no trolling sticks or jackpoles are visible. One of the vessels, about 36 feet long, has no pilot house—only a low trunk cabin over the engine. The other has a tiny deck house barely large enough to accommodate a helmsman.

Interesting boxlike structures are visible on the afterdecks. They must have been bait tanks, but they were very low, only knee high to the fishermen. Concern for hull stability was probably responsible for the low profile. No bait nets are to be seen so it is uncertain if they were actually using live bait in their fishing. It is possible that bait was obtained with a blanket net or from boats specializing in that business.

ALBACORE ON BAIT

Immigrant Japanese fishermen are credited with introducing the live bait and jackpole method of catching albacore—a type of fishing known to them for centuries. To excite tuna and conserve live bait, they simulated the splashing of bait fish by flicking the water with a tuft of feathers fixed to the end of a light pole. A perforated tin cup on a stick was another tool for sprinkling droplets on the surface. Feather and bone jigs, barbless "squids" ("strikers" to Yankee fishermen) and the bamboo poles used in the tuna industry for 50 years were all imported from Japan.

To trap live bait, Japanese fishermen employed a net similar to the crowders used to concentrate fish in receivers. Introduced in 1910, the blanket net was nearly the length of the boat. Two long poles were lashed to the net. Operators at each end of the boat would lower the poles under the surface and hold them nearly parallel. Minnows were chummed over the net and, when a school was attracted, the poles were raised. The fish were gathered in the bag of webbing between the poles and transferred to the tank. Only small amounts of bait were taken in blankets, but it made pole fishing feasible and catches of tuna increased accordingly. Bait tanks were only about knee high and fresh sea water was bailed in with a bucket dipped over the side. This wasn't as difficult as it sounds as the boats had a low freeboard and were not fast-moving.

Handlining albacore with live bait.

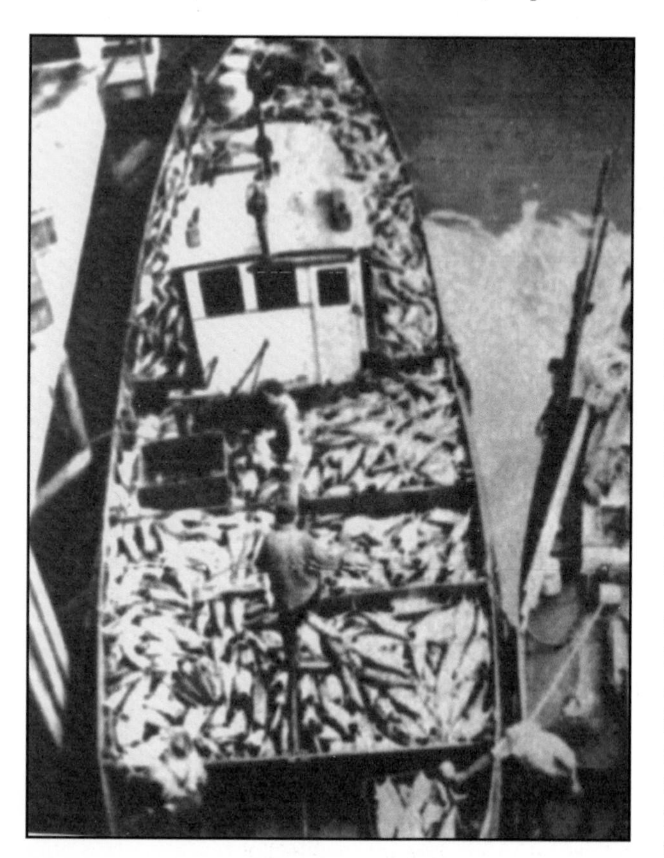

Deck filled with tons of albacore. This boat may have been acting as a tender for a buying barge.

The Italian roundhaul net, or lampara, was first used in 1912 and continued to be standard for catching bait until the appearance of the reeled purse nets now used. Larger tanks and increased bait capacity were made possible by new engine-driven pumps.

There is no more exciting fishing to be had than catching fast-biting tuna on a striker pole, but if their weight exceeds 25 pounds it can turn strenuous in a short time. For example, the high points of a 17-day trip in 1955 were two fabulous days outside the San Benitos. On three occasions we used a merry-go-round tactic on biting schools. With the engine in gear at reduced speed the wheel was lashed hard over so that the boat moved in a continuous circle. The skipper chummed as his son and I manned the racks. As I had the hot corner on the inside of the circle, strikes came instantly. Working our short poles and barbless squids, we threw albacore aboard in a steady stream. We put on over 200 plump longfins each time. A nearby boat described our action on radio as fish falling aboard "like silver rain."

If the fish are wary it is often necessary to use a baited hook rather than the feathered squid. One of the finest exhibitions of fishing skill I ever saw was provided by a real pro of Portuguese persuasion. Using a bait pole, he was "winging" each 20-pound albacore he hooked. As he yanked a fish from the water he caught it under his left arm and held it immobilized, meanwhile dropping the butt of the pole between his feet. Cradling the pole with his elbow, he extracted the hook with his right hand. The unhooked albie was thrust backwards to drop on deck and the fisherman was ready to rebait his hook and repeat the process.

Earliest type bait boats, 1916.

It was a totally macho performance, but it was executed with such smooth coordination that it looked nearly effortless. Except with small fish, I never had the temerity to try it. Usually, I dropped them on deck and gripped them by the eyeballs while removing the hook. Japanese tuna fishermen are longtime experts at "winging" and learn the skill as small boys in fishing school, practicing with a stuffed cloth imitation fish attached to a long pole.

A typical bait boat in 1914 was about 40 feet long, driven with a 15 to 25 HP gas engine and cost about $2,500 to build. Crew averaged three men. Many boats brought in from four to six tons of albacore on their one-day local trips and anything less than a ton was considered poor fishing. By 1925 larger boats, called "albacore chasers," of 45 to 60 feet powered with 80 HP engines were numerous. Most original open party sport boats were conversions of these types

ALBACORE ON JIGS

When albacore were abundant and close by, schools were worked by hundreds of small trolling boats. The vessels had only a basic round bottomed displacement hull, gasoline engine and box compass. Fancy electronic and mechanical aids were nonexistent. The fish were brought in the same day, or sometimes iced on a two-day trip. Jigboats peaked in numbers during the years 1920-25 and took at least 50 percent of the supply for canning.

Hauling in an albacore hand over hand while the boat is moving at a fast troll is similar to towing a bucket. The fish always attempt to sound, but if they drag until exhausted they will sometimes ski along the surface. If the bite is steady and the fish are large, hand pulling can become arduous indeed. Painful cramps often develop in hands and arms. To lessen finger abrasion a circular hand grip of grooved rubber was sometimes worn. Many fishermen found it awkward and settled instead for cotton work gloves. Nowadays all professional trollers have mechanical line pullers to relieve the strain of heavy hauling.

Modern lines are of braided nylon or other synthetics whereas the cords of yore were usually 72 to 108-thread hard laid cotton seine twine, tanned or dyed blue or green. Tarred hemp cordage was also used. Methods of rigging the gear varied according to the whims of individual fishermen; some tapering the lines and others using them level to the leader. To connect the two-foot wire leader, a pigtail swivel was eyespliced to the tip of each line. Hooks long ago were coated with black enamel and later tinned or zinc dipped. After WW II, barbless hooks of stainless steel became available and are now universally favored. In the earliest days of the troll fishery homemade lures, cedar plugs, lampwick jigs and sometimes spoons were used. Japanese style bone and feather lures eventually superseded the others and remain favorites today.

The number of lines trolled varied from six to 14 depending on boat size and length of outrigger poles. Lines were staggered in length so long, unweighted ones could be pulled over the shorter, or weighted, lines and retrieved up the center of the boat's wake. During a hot bite the long lines would be left on deck and only the shorter ones returned to the water. Even so, tangles were common when lines were loading. Care had to be taken that enough jigs remained in the water to keep following albacore interested.

Jigs were sometimes grabbed by marlin or mako sharks and I have seen outrigger poles snapped by these heavyweights. Bringing in all lures was often the only way to get rid of an excited marlin.

A warm water influx in 1926 caused a drastic drop in catches. For seven years (1928-34) albacore fishing was a

The author with albacore and tuna, 1938.

complete failure and jigboats were forced into other fisheries. In 1942 the fish reappeared in numbers and there was another large increase in the troller fleet. For the past twenty years there has been a steady and continuing decline in the number of small boats. Vessels surviving in the fishery today have labor-saving and seakeeping improvements undreamed of 60 years ago. So sturdy and sophisticated are modern commercial craft that a midocean albacore troll fishery has been developed. Centered between Midway Island and Dutch Harbor, Alaska, this fishery is currently expanding into the South Pacific

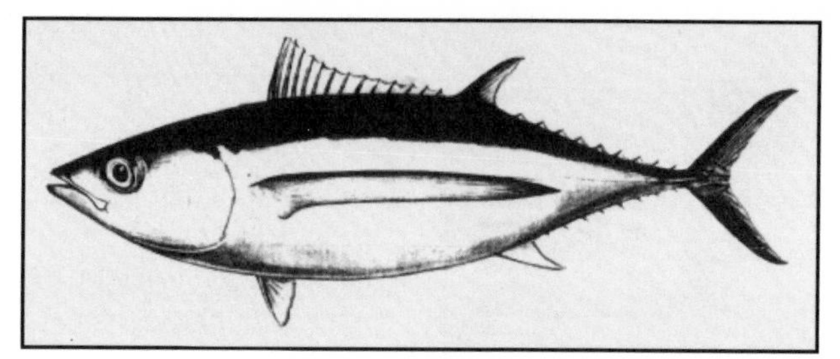

Albacore, the chicken of the sea.

LONGFIN FACTS

It is difficult to imagine the vast numbers of fish present in coastal waters eighty years ago. The inshore migration of albacore from 1916 to 1926 must have been tremendous. The annual catch fell below 12.5 million pounds only three times and peaked in 1917 when 30.6 million pounds were landed. That was an estimated minimum of 1.5 million albacore taken between the Mexican border and Pt. Conception. Larger total catches have since been made, notably in 1951 when 62 million pounds were landed. However, the bulk of that tonnage was taken off Mexico. Alas, it is unlikely that such fishing will ever be seen again.

Reason for the seemingly erratic behavior of the fish was a mystery until intensive research in the 1950s found that migration routes are determined by water temperature gradients, 60 to 67 degrees being the preferred range. Smaller scattered fish (jig fish) are in colder water while larger, more tightly schooled fish (bait fish) are apt to be in the warmer ranges. Albacore are the world's migratory champs, travelling from the mid-Pacific spawning grounds to our coast at an average 17 miles per day and achieving 16 miles daily on their way to Japan. After they enter our coastal fishery they turn northward, moving about six miles a day near the coast and 15 offshore. Tagging studies have shown little mixing between the southern California population and the fish that appear off Oregon.

Albacore do not reproduce until they are about six years old. With few exceptions, none of the fish caught locally have spawned. Albies grow fast, doubling in size every year until maturity. One year-olds average 6½ pounds and reach 13 pounds in two years, and 20 pounds at three. The 60-pound giants that were caught in the fall of 1984 were six to eight years old.

Bait boats at the cannery pier.

Waiting to unload.

The albacore fleet, bait boats and trollers, at Fish Harbor, San Pedro, c. 1917.

"Monterey" type albacore jig boats.

"Pulling albacore," from a painting by the author.

Boating a jigged albacore.

COLUMBUS on the bait grounds. Tanks are filled, after deck at water level and racks folded in until fishing commences. A makeshift pipe and canvas canopy shades the after tank. Small boat is used for bait catching.

"Four-pole teamwork," from a painting by the author

Chapter 11
THE TUNA CHASE

In 1926, for the first time since the founding of the canned tuna industry, albacore failed to appear off the California coast. Fishermen and canners alike were desperate. Small jigboats were forced to tie up or enter other fisheries. Larger bait boats searched to the southward for the elusive longfins. The explorers found no albacore, but yellowfin tuna and skipjack were plentiful in Mexican waters. Over the next few years the latter species supplanted albacore as the basic raw material for tuna canning.

Albacore chaser bait boats were under 60 feet, mostly gas powered, and limited in range and carrying capacity. On the desolate Mexican coast, suitable operating bases for such vessels were nonexistent. The predicament was addressed by stationing cannery mother ships at Turtle Bay, Cedros Island and Magdalena Bay. Resupply and retransport of fish meant high overhead and reduced earnings for fishermen and canners alike. A solution was found in new boats capable of long-range fishing and delivering catches directly to the canneries. The development of the tuna clipper resulted in rapid increases in vessel size, range and cargo capacity.

From the start, obtaining live bait was a major concern. Precious days were often spent in a vain search for bait schools. Magdalena Bay, Banderas Bay, the Gulf of Fonseca and the Gulf of Nicoya in Costa Rica were prime bait grounds. Any small fish were usable for tuna bait, but anchovetas and sardines were preferred. A large clipper could carry 1,000 scoops of bait in her huge tanks. At first, bait net setting and hauling was from the stern of the clippers. As vessels grew in size and draft it became necessary to carry a skiff and motorboat for bait catching.

Aboard tuna boats the chummer was an important person. Responsibility for the care and feeding of bait fish was his primary duty. The small fish were fed with finely-ground skipjack or corn meal. To prevent contamination, dead baits were regularly siphoned from tank bottoms. Modern bait tank design and water circulation formulas are the result of knowledge gained on tuna clippers.

Fishing was carried out with Japanese-made lures, feather-dressed barbless hooks mounted in "brass pipe squids," attached to bamboo poles by a short line and wire leader. Tuna were chummed to a feeding frenzy and yanked aboard in a steady stream, with a good day's catch amounting to 40 tons or more. Long range anglers who have seen hot schools of biting yellowfin can easily comprehend the frantic pace of such fishing.

The larger the fish, the more power it took to heave them aboard, so two or more poles and lines were bridled to one leader. Tuna from 40 to 60 pounds were two-pole fish, 60 to 90 pounders were three-polers and 90 to 120 pounders

A thick pad over the groin was used to prevent injury from pole thrust.

were four-polers. This strenuous and exciting method of fishing is now practically obsolete for American boats. Only a few small bait boats still operate in the fishery. Fiberglass poles have replaced the bamboos. Long range sportfishers and seiners now cruise the banks first discovered by pioneering tunamen.

When the fish stopped biting, no rest ensued for the fishermen. Donning oilskins, they descended from tropical heat to the frigid hold for icing down. Often working on all fours or sprawled belly down in the cramped bins, they carefully packed tuna in alternating layers of fish and ice. If the day's catch was large, this backbreaking toil could go on for many hours. The chilled brine system, introduced in 1936, eventually eliminated such arduous methods of preserving the catch. Fish were merely dropped through deck hatches into brine wells fitted in each side of the hold.

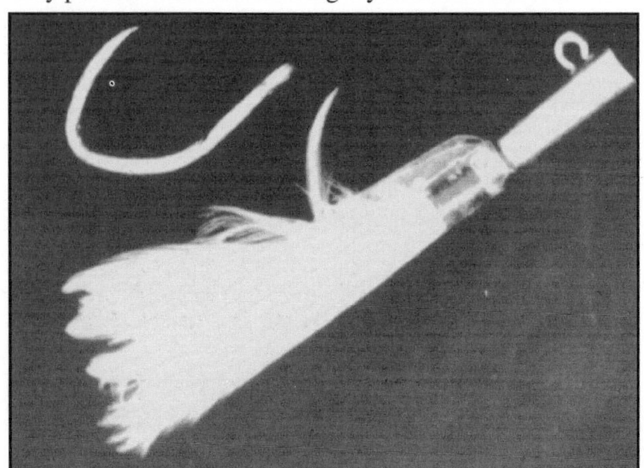

Bait hook and "squid," or "striker."

TUNA HAZARDS

Live bait and jackpole tuna fishing was an interesting and adventurous way of making a living from the sea, but it was not without its occupational hazards. Crippled backs, ruptures, and disfiguring abrasions that came with catching a heavy fish square in the face, were commonplace. Flying hooks, splintered poles, beating fish tails and snapping teeth caused cuts and punctures galore. Terrible bruising around the men's groins resulted from the thrust of the poles when lifting heavy fish. At first, quilted canvas aprons were sewn together and faced with a horseshoe of heavy rope to contain the pole butts. These were eventually replaced by the thick leather pads with deep sockets still used today.

Usually, tuna in a school vary but little in size. When fishing one-polers, an occasional large fish was hooked. The unlucky fisherman would be in for a hard time, often being jerked overboard. Quick action by his fellows was needed to effect a rescue.

Beware of leaping wahoo. From a painting by the author.

On one occasion a large wahoo, chasing chum laid for tuna, became airborne and smashed into a startled fisherman. Sharp jaws ripped the man's face so severely that emergency evacuation by the Coast Guard was required. Anglers familiar with wahoo can imagine the terrible trauma inflicted by the fish's razor teeth.

During a pause in the fishing, Captain Joe Monise of the INVADER noticed the baitboy was absent from his perch atop the tank. He might have been in another part of the ship, but some hunch caused Monise to leap to the tank top and look inside. Thousands of live sardines formed a nearly solid mass as they milled on the surface. The skipper was about to turn away when he glimpsed a straw hat below the swarming bait. Two desperately groping hands seized his deep-dipped arm and a moment later the half-drowned baitboy lay sputtering and gasping on the deck. A few seconds more and INVADER would have made a sad passage homeward carrying a gruesome cargo in the ice hold.

As tuna flopped on the deck, blood poured from the scuppers attracting hordes of sharks. In a feeding frenzy, sharks snapped at squids and hooked fish. In heavy swells a boat could roll her rails under until the fishermen were armpit deep in the water. It was not unknown for a shark to be caught in a fishing rack on the upward roll—a very dangerous situation. To give their shipmates a short respite, fishermen would sometimes tempt sharks away from the racks by towing a hooked tuna around the bow.

Sanoshike Ueno of the clipper ALERT, attempting to gaff a seven-foot shark entrapped in the bait net, had his hand severely mangled. The writhing monster, twisting and snapping, bit off a finger. Infection developed and the wounded man was rushed back to port and hospitalized, but too late to prevent death from lockjaw.

The chummer was an important person aboard tuna boats.

One-pole tuna fishing. Man in foreground is using a live bait.

Sharks were not the only hazard. While serving as engineer in the clipper LUSITANIA, Tony Rosa attempted to gaff a marlin that was spooking the tuna. Straddling the rail, Rosa leaned out to sink home the gaff. Losing his balance, he plunged downward at the same moment the marlin lunged forward. Its spiked bill rammed through Rosa's thigh into the wooden hull. Fortunately, the bill broke off but Tony was nailed to the hull. After rescue, he feared septic poisoning and insisted on having an iodine swab passed through the wound. Not long after, this rugged man arose and limped below to tend his engines.

Banderas Bay is home to poisonous sea snakes and a swarm of the reptiles once clogged the bait tank intakes of a clipper that was curing fresh-caught live sardines before heading for offshore banks. The captain was beside himself at the prospect of losing the bait and incurring further costly delays in an already lengthy trip. Clearing the snakes from the intake screens was the only way to restore water circulation and save the bait, but none of the fishermen would enter the snake-infested sea. The engineer, a man of courage, finally volunteered for the dangerous job. Donning a navy peacoat and watch cap, he pulled on two pairs of cotton gloves. A diving mask with air hose was fitted over his head and he plunged over the side and swam under the boat. Snakes were yanked from the strainer and the water flow was restored. For his daring act, the diver was rewarded with an extra half-share of profits at trip's end.

The greatest single danger to boats and men was the chubasco, the sudden savage storm that plagues the Central American coast. When the clipper NAVIGATOR was caught in one her pilot house was smashed and the captain and two crewmen were cut by flying glass. The motor launch was torn from its cradle and hurled back to the bait tank and then

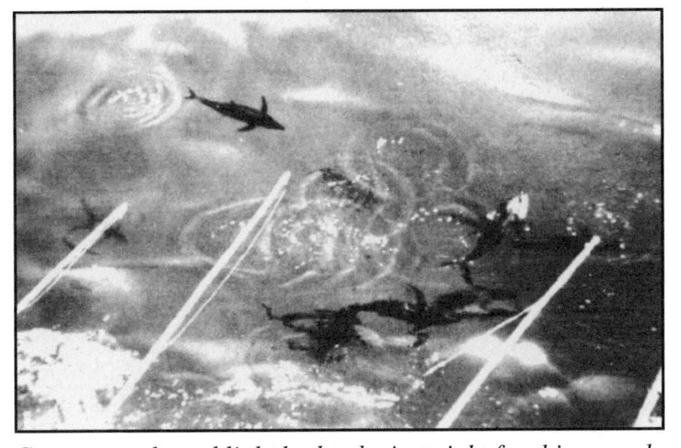

Camera angle and light had to be just right for this remarkable photo of tuna under the poles.

Large one-pole tuna is heaved aboard. Note squid dangling from pole at right.

to the lower deck. Every piece of gear above deck was washed away. The lights went out and the steering gear broke, but the sturdy vessel survived the hurricane and was patched up to fish another day.

One fisherman who ventured on deck during a storm was washed overboard. He remained alive by diving each time the mountainous waves broke over his head. It was an hour before the boat could turn during a lull and another hour before the exhausted swimmer was sighted. A shipmate, with a line tied around his waste, jumped into the sea and made the rescue.

Manuel Severiano was swept from the deck one night as the CABRILLO plunged through rough seas thirty miles off the Mexican coast. He found a hatch cover that came adrift at the same time and clung to it for four days. Chilled by night, roasted by day and constantly accompanied by sharks, he finally drifted ashore. Found and cared for by Mexican peasants, he was fishing again within two months.

Others were not so lucky. Every year, two to six boats were lost. Radar and Loran were nonexistent and the fishing areas had few navigational aids on their desolate shores. Groundings and collisions with uncharted reefs were frequent. The BELLE ISLE disappeared without trace in the Gulf of Panama; the VANTUNA capsized on her maiden voyage; the ST. VERONICA was wrecked in the Galapagos; the LOIS S. struck a reef and sank; the CONTINENTAL burned off Cocos Island and the OLYMPIA exploded off Cabo San Lucas. Such was the toll of disasters attending the pursuit of tuna.

Two poles are bridled to one leader and hook for bigger fish.

Heavy tuna puts a strain on three poles.

FORGOTTEN BANKS

Prospecting for albacore in 1928, the new 72-foot boat UNCLE SAM had wandered some 450 miles south from San Diego. An area swarming with seals and bird life 60 miles off the Baja coast led Captain Frank Silva to order soundings to be taken. A weighted line was dropped and, sure enough, shoal water was found. Thus, the Uncle Sam Bank discovered. During the growth years of the tuna industry, thousands of tons of yellowfin and skipjack were taken on and near this spot.

Silva kept to himself the location of the bank he discovered, but it was not long before the secret was out and during a good run of tuna 20 to 40 vessels at one time could be found fishing there.

In the early years of its exploitation exceptionally large tuna, up to 350 pounds, were found on the Uncle Sam Bank.

CHALLENGER and other clippers served with distinction as navy patrol craft in World War II.

Live bait was used but outboard racks had not yet been invented and fishing was done from the stern deck. To aid in boating large fish, bulwarks were cut to six inches around the stern. Bridling poles together to form two, three and four-pole sets was still in the future. After years of catching the smaller albacore on single poles, methods for boating giant yellowfin were still experimental.

Armed with a large hook and heavy wire leader, a heavy rope-like line was attached to a short six-foot bamboo pole. A live sardine on the hook usually produced a strike. Three men holding the pole would pull the thrashing tuna as close as possible to the boat. A fourth man was standing by with a large gaff hook fixed to an eight to ten foot pole. The fish was hooked in the head and all four men wrestled the tuna aboard. This awkward, labor intensive and downright dangerous method was eliminated by the invention of outboard fishing racks and multiple-pole rigs.

All the banks and island hot spots visited by our long range sportfishing fleet were first discovered or fished in the 1920s and '30s by exploring tuna boats.

Built in 1929, Captain Harold Morgan's 122-foot clipper CHICKEN OF THE SEA was one of the first to be equipped with a submarine signal fathometer. The newfangled electronic gizmo proved its worth on her maiden voyage. The famous Morgan Bank was discovered and produced such fishing that the boat was able to make three full-load fares of yellowfin, totalling 452 tons, in about 40 days. Morgan's mortgage was paid off in record time.

Newfound banks were named for the discovering boat or skipper. The Lusitania, Golden Gate, Picaroto and Paramount banks were named for vessels. The Lou Brito, Rosa and Morgan Banks for captains, and so on.

As the tuna vessels grew in size and fuel capacity, they worked ever further to the south and east searching for bonanza fishing. More new banks were discovered. By 1930 a few boats had ventured as far as Panama and the Galapagos Islands. The Navigator Bank off Cape Mala, Panama was found by Manuel Neves, and the Normandie Bank was located 75 miles south of the Galapagos by Captain Joe Marques.

The Cadillac Bank, 175 miles north of the Galapagos, was one site named neither for a boat nor a skipper. The designation resulted from the luxury cars crewmen were able to purchase with large shares earned on fast, full-load trips to the new hot spot.

The almost mythical Allaire Bank was the object of repeated searches, all in vain. In 1916 a merchant vessel claimed it had been able to easily anchor 700 miles off the Mexican coast, far west and slightly north of Clarion Island. What the fishermen did find there were severe storms, and eventually the area was avoided. The so-called Hurricane Bank may be the current identity of the "lost" shoal.

In 1930 Captain John Hansen of the clipper GLENN MAYNE declared he had located the elusive bank. He brought in 190 tons of tuna, largest fare landed to that date. Fishing captains were notorious for misinformation and secretiveness about the location of a successful catch. Since nobody else had good luck there, it is possible that his big haul was made at another spot. In those days there was usually only one navigator aboard capable of determining the ship's position by sextant sights. Sometimes these were paper captains hired solely for that skill. If there were no visible landmarks, ordinary crewmen often had only a vague idea where they were fishing.

Pop Morgan's CHICKEN OF THE SEA.

ORIENT was first steel-hulled clipper.

NAVIGATOR carried a spotting seaplane atop her tank canopy.

Early tuna boat ABRAHAM LINCOLN

Catching two-pole tuna from AMERICAN BEAUTY, from a painting by the author.

The photo on the previous page shows the CHALLENGER on her trial run. She is a typical tuna clipper of the late 1930s. Ranging in length from 120 to 150 feet in length, the boats were heavily built of wood and carried up to 350 tons fish. A single 500 HP heavy duty diesel drove the hull while a pair of auxiliaries provided power for pumps and electricity. Not shown in the photo are the steel racks that hung around the stern outside the bulwarks to provide a platform for the men while fishing.

The most conspicuous feature of the tuna boats was the huge bait tank resting on the afterdeck. The 115-foot YANKEE carried a tank whose dimensions were 29' x 17' x 6'. The amount of water contained was tremendous, amounting in a typical case to 140 tons, which supported up to 1,000 scoops of live bait. Also notable was the almost total absence of freeboard aft. When loaded with bait and fuel a boat's afterdeck was awash, or nearly so, and the resultant stability problems led to a number of disasters from capsizings and founderings. Tropical storms encountered on the fishing banks wracked the overloaded vessels and the excessive weights fore and aft caused terrific hogging strains in the wooden hulls.

The large live bait tuna clipper began to vanish from the scene after 1960 when synthetic seine twine and the power block made possible the use of huge nets. The purse seine depends not on the biting whims of fish.

In 1980 the canneries began closing their West Coast facilities and relocating to cheap labor areas. Since then over 12,500 jobs have been lost and the dollar losses in wages, sales and tax revenues runs into billions. The demise of the tuna industry is an unpleasant fact affecting even sportfishermen in a minor way since it has caused difficulties in getting their tuna catches processed. In early 1985 it was known that 26 percent of U.S. seiners, 10 percent of U.S. bait boats and 25 percent of U.S. trollers were idle because they could not operate at a profit or find a market for their catch.

There are no survivors of the wooden clipper fleet. The newer ones were pressed into naval service during World War II and served with distinction as minesweepers or island supply runners. After the war most new construction was in steel and all suitable hulls were converted to seining in the 1960's. Some readers may remember the hulk of the old ZARCO, ex-CHICKEN OF THE SEA, lingering on in San Diego Bay until she was sunk as a derelict. She was the last of the wooden clippers.

This chapter is dedicated to my friend the late Captain Anthony Mascarenhas, a salty toiler of the sea who was proud of the tuna clippers and their contribution to San Diego's history and economy.

Tons of three-pole tuna fill the deck to capacity.

Fishermen take a well-earned break. Pole butts rest in live bait hand wells.

Clipper fishing on the banks.

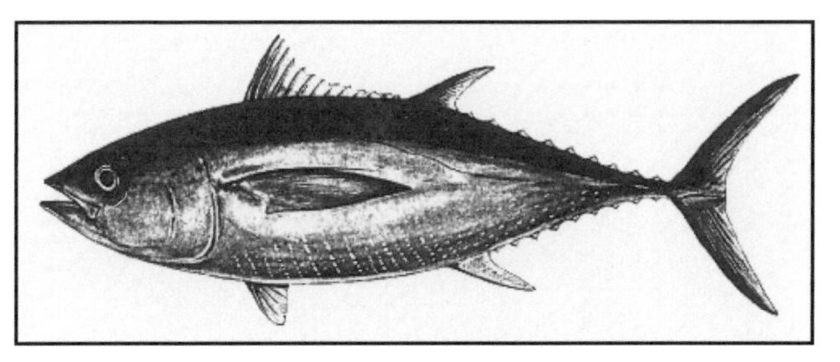

Object of the chase: Yellowfin tuna.

"Fishing in the '30s," from a painting by the author.

Bob Oefinger's Ocean Park all-day boat RAMONA fishing near Rocky Point, 1938.

Part V

PIONEERS AND PERSONALITIES

Chapter 12

A MIXED BAG

COLORFUL CHARACTERS

As a young fishing fanatic, I spent every possible moment on the Santa Monica pier. Residing a mere four blocks away, it was easy to put in considerable time there. It was soon apparent there were many other regular visitors to that fascinating place. Some of them made a lasting impression.

For instance, there was the barrel-shaped lady that specialized in perch fishing. She reminded me of Tugboat Annie, feisty heroine of the Saturday Evening Post stories by Norman Reilly Raine. She was cantankerous and opinionated, but kind enough to show me the correct way to open and shuck a mussel: "You put the knife point in where the tuft of hair comes out between the shells." She and another old-timer once quarreled loudly over the identity of a sargo he had caught. "Chinese croaker" and "Japanese croaker" were common names then applied to black croaker and sargo. The argument raged over which was appropriate for the catch in question. It remains a mystery how those Asian appellations were derived in the first place. The lady became cold toward me after I had the temerity to doubt her opinion that sultry, humid weather was a cause of earthquakes.

The halibut expert was an aged African-American who fished always at the same spot in the middle of the south side of the pier. He used homemade cane poles with rusty guides of twisted wire wrapped on with friction tape. His reels were wooden sidewinders and the rigs were secured to the pier railing on ingenious rod holders made of scrap lumber and cord. Despite his crude equipment, if flatfish were to be had the old man always scored.

Then there was a gent I called the Corbina Man. A taciturn loner, he was rumored to be a shell-shocked veteran of the first world war. Dressed always in the same olive drab army surplus clothing, he used an Eastern-type surf rod of split bamboo with over-and-under guides and a long hickory "spring butt." Huge gobs of fresh mussels, wrapped to the hooks with silk thread, were his preferred baits. If not tramping the beaches he could often be found fishing from the south side of the pier behind the ballroom, an area with little foot traffic. He caught more corbina and croaker than anybody I ever saw, but he avoided company and would move on if someone fished within a hundred feet of him. A surly grunt was the only reply I ever got from him in response to my questions. I learned to keep a respectful silence and study his technique as unobtrusively as possible.

In the 1930s a long, upward-slanting extension, minus handrails, was attached to the end of the pier. Built as a construction bridge to the projected breakwater, it was never used for that purpose. Access was fenced off, but resourceful anglers found a way around the barrier. An expert handline fisherman was often to be found at the extreme end. His method was to whirl an eight ounce sinker around his head and let it fly, carrying his coiled handline a considerable distance. Two or three leaders with live bait would be snapped to the knotless cord and allowed to slide, trolley

The Earthquake Lady.

fashion, down the line. He was very successful with halibut, bonito and barracuda, occasionally bringing in two fish at once.

Once a week a little gray-haired lady came to the landing and wheedled a free ride in the shoreboat to the STAR OF SCOTLAND barge. There she filled two gallon jugs with clean offshore sea water from the bait tank. She believed a few briny sips taken daily had great therapeutic and medicinal value.

Riding the live bait boats was another group of regulars. Roly-poly, white-moustached Old Joe, came every Thursday. In addition to his own catch, he would buy for a penny a pound all the barracuda I could capture. Others became familiar by such handles as Ace, Tin Bucket, Parson, Dynamite, Fatty, Tadpole, Deacon, Blackie, etc. Oldtime skippers I remember were Abe and Dick Gregory, Bill Lightfoot, Joe Fudge, Orrin Winfield, Sam Anderson and Tom Hernage. There were many more, of course, characters whose faces and names were familiar to me then. I recall them all with delight for the color and interest they brought to a pleasant time in my life.

CAPTAIN T. J. MORRIS

Gale force winds and high seas recall a time when such storms invariably meant disaster for fishing fleets operating from exposed piers, particularly in Santa Monica Bay. Real tragedy was sometimes a result. Captain Thornton J. Morris, a retired owner and master of sailing ships, settled in Santa Monica at the end of the first world war. He purchased a pair of commercial launches, the URSULA and the JOSIE M., and opened a pleasure fishing business on the municipal pier. He was one of the first to offer mobile, open party boats running on a regular basis. By 1926 Morris had a fleet of six live bait boats. When not operating, they were secured to buoys set in the open sea.

During a gale on Feb. 13th, the new Morris boat AMECO broke from her mooring and smashed into the pier, battering herself to pieces. It was an agonizing loss to her owner. Record high seas and huge breakers were kicked up by another violent storm onApril 8th, 1926. The entire South Coast was strewn with wreckage. Seven boats sank or were driven ashore at Santa Monica and barges were beached at Redondo and Newport.

All morning Morris and his employees anxiously observed the boats plunging and jerking at their exposed moorings a quarter mile off the end of the pier. A little after noon the 50-foot W. K. parted her chain and began a rapid drift towards the pier. Determined to make a try at saving the launch, Morris hooked a 16-foot skiff to the pierhead der-

The Corbina Man.

Morris' first AMECO. Note lifeboat on davits.

rick. Manning the rowboat with two volunteer crewmen, Leo Gregory and Paul Brooks, he gave the order to lower away. Ignoring the advice of bystanders, the men wore no life-jackets. The captain's many years of seafaring experience may have made him overconfident, but he evidently felt that wearing clumsy cork jackets would hinder vigorous rowing.

On the back of a series of great swells, the skiff was swiftly lowered into the seething sea. Rowing strongly, the courageous trio cleared the pier and headed for the W. K. Watchers frequently lost sight of the little craft in the wave troughs, but at last it was seen to be nearing the derelict vessel. With only fifty feet to go, an enormous breaker capsized the skiff. Floundering in a welter of foam, the three men struggled to reach the overturned boat.

As the grim drama unfolded, two young men on the pier prepared to launch a second skiff for an immediate rescue attempt. They were Jack Duggan, a son-in-law of Morris, and Charles Terasi, both employed by the captain. Pausing only long enough to don lifejackets, and with three more in the boat, they lowered away safely and set off. Now but two of the first crew were intermittently visible. Captain Morris was seen spread full length on the bottom of his skiff, striving desperately to pull Paul Brooks up beside him. Buried by tons of water, they too disappeared.

Moments later, huge rollers overwhelmed the two gallant boys in the rescue craft. Saved from the crashing surf by their cork jackets and the valiant efforts of lifeguards, they barely escaped with their lives. The dying Leo Gregory was recovered from beneath Crystal Pier, but the bodies of Morris and Brooks were not found. Ironically, the W. K., after washing up on the beach, was later salvaged and lived to fish another day.

An enormous breaker...

Before his demise, Morris spent much time and energy trying to bring a breakwater to Santa Monica. The miserable rockpile that was built nine years later was a far cry from the high, piertopped enclosure that was the captain's dream.

Perhaps it is just as well that Captain Morris passed on when he did as further terrible mishaps were in store for his little fleet. The boat FASHION, with 45 passengers aboard, burned to the water's edge on June 9th, 1927. No lives were lost, but it represented a grievous financial setback. The worst was yet to come. Three years later a Morris boat was involved in one of the most dreadful accidents ever to befall a sportfishing vessel.

Aboard MINNIE A. CAINE.

On Memorial Day, 1930, the new AMECO capsized and sank with the loss of 16 lives. Such a tragedy would surely have broken the captain's stout heart.

Few people today remember Morris' pioneering contribution to sportfishing and the dogged battle he fought against the misfortune that beset him.

"SANTA MONICA OLSEN"

Perhaps the most colorful character ever to be involved with the sportfishing industry was Captain Olaf C. Olsen. Known as "Cap" to his friends, he operated a small fleet of boats and barges from the Santa Monica Pier during the peak of that landing's popularity as a fishing port. Olsen was born in Norway and as a boy went to sea in sailing ships. His original family name was Krog. After a row with a mate, he jumped ship in Pensacola. An American shipping clerk, unable to spell the name correctly, declared that "All Scandinavians are named Olsen." So Olsen he remained ever after—according to one of the tales he told of himself. In the 1890s, after rounding Cape Horn in a square-rigger, he landed in San Francisco. Serving in the lumber carriers sailing from West Coast ports, he became a "bucko mate," enforcing discipline among deckhands with fists and belaying pins. Olsen claimed he was the only man to beat

Captain Olaf Olsen.

across Oregon's dangerous Humbolt Bar in a "two masted schooner during a howlin' southeaster." Before settling in Santa Monica, he operated a series of lumber tugs in the Northwest.

In March 1925 Olsen bought the old whaling bark NARWHAL and set her up as a fishing barge. As the masts were still standing, her excessive rolling often caused seasickness. Instead of cutting the sticks out of her, he sold her for movie work. In 1927 Cap purchased the three masted schooner FOX from the Wm. Fox Vaudeville Co. Originally the ALLEN A, she was built in 1888 and was a fur trader in the Arctic. With her masts cut down the FOX was a stable and popular fishing platform. So successful was she that a second schooner, the CHARLES BROWN, was bought. She

MINNIE A. CAINE stranded at Topanga. 1939.

was a 76-footer, formerly the Japanese sealer TOKAI MARU, built in 1904 and evidently seized for poaching in Alaskan waters. To service the barges, several powerboats were acquired. The GLORIA H. was used as a tug to shift the barges to new fishing spots, doubling occasionally as an all-day partyboat. The ORIOLE and VIKING provided taxi service to the barges. HAROLD O. and VIKING also served on charter and open party runs. The boats were operated by Olsen's sons, Harold and Einar, and longtime skipper Bob Le Beau.

The business continued to thrive and in May 1931 the large four masted schooner MINNIE A. CAINE was added to the fleet. Joan Lowell wrote a novel, *Cradle of the Deep*, about her real and imagined life as a child aboard the ship. The book was lampooned by another writer with a story entitled *Salt Water Taffy*. Captain Olsen would chuckle tolerantly at the obvious errors in the first book and roar with laughter at the second in which the heroine struggled to avoid being bitten by "copras" in the ship's cargo.

Cap was very popular and well-known in the decade before the war. For his enthusiastic boosting of bay fishing a newspaper dubbed him "Santa Monica Olsen." Always ready with a story pitched in a heavy Norwegian accent, he was the epitome of a salty sailing ship seaman. Stocky and powerful in build, he always wore a sailor's billed cap and smoked a pipe. Married five times, he was capable of considerable rugged charm and was the model for Popeye, the comic strip character.

Olsen's VIKING served as barge shoreboat and charter craft.

Olsen's toughest challenge came on September 24, 1939 when a southeast gale drove the MINNIE A. CAINE ashore near Topanga Canyon. Piloting a 40 HP tug, he and son Harold strove desperately to hold her off the beach. Tossed by fifty-foot waves, Einar, five other men and a dog rode the barge into the surf. In the cabin a piano came adrift and crashed about like a loose cannon.

Salvaging the old schooner was impractical. As tears rolled down Cap's face, the old schooner was burnt where she lay. Of Olsen's barges only FOX remained. Moved to Long Beach during the war, she served briefly as a postwar barge before ending up in Mexico. Olsen retired and was 70 when he passed away in June 1950. None who met him are likely to forget the colorful old sea dog.

Robert J. Oefinger, the fishing druggist.

THE FISHING DRUGGIST

One of the best-known sportfishing entrepreneurs of the era between world wars was Robert F. J. Oefinger, self-styled Commodore of a small flotilla of boats and barges operating in Santa Monica Bay. Bob, as this friendly gent was known to all, was born in Meriden, Connecticut in 1886 and educated as a chemist. For many years he worked as manager and owner of a series of Owl Drug stores in the Los Angeles area. As a longtime recreational fisherman, he was quick to see the potential of the booming ocean sport.

Selling out his drug store business in 1928, Bob and partner Max Watt bought a pair of boats and began operations as Santa Monica Pleasure Fishing Boats, Inc. FREEDOM and COLLEEN, running half and all day trips, were soon joined by charter boat LOIS. Faced with stiff competition at Santa Monica, Oefinger in 1929 signed a ten-year lease and shifted his landing to the Ocean Park fishing pier.

GEORGE E. BILLINGS, a former five-masted schooner, was acquired for barge service. Built in 1903, she was dismantled in San Diego in 1926 and refitted as a barge. Due to Bob's promotional efforts the "Big Barge BILLINGS" became famous and popular. On her arrival off the pier, he led a crew of pretty girls, dressed as pirates, to "capture" prominent members of the Ocean Park Business Men's Association. The captives were hauled out to the barge where more high jinks ensued as the men were initiated into the Sacred Order of Salt Water Anglers. Oefinger then extended an invitation, via the newspapers, for a free day of fishing on the barge. Such stunts paid off handsomely.

The excellent fishing to be had in those days also contributed to the success of the enterprise. Oefinger and Watt fished often, concentrating on black seabass. They caught many of the giant fish and lost no opportunity to publicize their feats in newspapers. Pier fishing was good, too, with a catch of over 600 white sea bass taken in one night. Charles Ely, a regular on the pier, landed 240 halibut in one season and hauls of over 2,000 barracuda were made in one day by the live bait boats.

By the mid-'thirties a second barge, the BAITWELL, had been added to the fleet and RAMONA had replaced COLLEEN. FREEDOM ran halfdays, ORCA was the bait boat and MARDI GRAS serviced the barges. A photo of the RAMONA shows her fishing off Rocky Point in July, 1938. She was diesel powered and rather advanced for her time with a much larger deckhouse than was usual on local sportboats. Note the anglers balancing atop the benches to avoid wet feet caused by the boat's low freeboard. Most of the sacks have a fish or two in them and more are stowed under the bench seats. Dangling from the bow is a rope stringer and draped over the rail is the heavy springline used to hold the boat alongside the pier. The skipper waves a pop bottle as he leans on the bait tank while the lad by the life ring strikes a jaunty pose.

In September 1940 the barge OLYMPIC II was run down and sunk by a Japanese steamer off San Pedro, with a loss of eight lives. Before the end of the year a law was enforced applying strict regulations for bulkheading in barges. It was impossible for old sailing vessels to comply without complete rebuilding and most were forced to cease operating. Faced with $500 a day in fines for noncompliance, Oefinger had the BILLINGS, valued at $26,000, towed to one of the Channel Islands. There she was beached and put to the torch. Disgusted and discouraged, Bob retired from the fishing business, but returned to the waterfront for a wartime stint in the Coast Guard Auxiliary. Mourned by his hundreds of fishing friends, he passed away in January, 1956.

Promotional activities aboard barge BILLINGS.

NEWPORT SKIPPER

It was the summer of 1940 when I first became acquainted with Sammy Cordeiro. He was skippering the SUN SHINE II out of King's Landing in Newport Beach and I was for a time his deckhand. He was a young fellow, not much older than I, but already a seasoned fisherman. As a boy he had fished in the famous dory fleet with his father, surfing out beside the pier to longline for rockfish and halibut.

In 1931 Sam went to work for the Ozene brothers as second deck on the live bait boats SUNSHINE and WOLFMAN operating from Newport Pier. Darrell King bought out the Ozenes in 1933 and added the VALENCIAS to the fleet. Sam continued to work for King and in 1938 obtained his operator's license.

After the great storm of 1939 wrecked the Newport pier, King acquired a large bayside property next to the Lido Isle bridge. There he built a cafe and office, put in slips and bait receivers, and resumed operations from a sheltered location.

During my time with him Sam introduced me to most of the Orange County fishing hot spots. On the SUNSHINE II we left at 0200 and made the long jaunt to San Onofre and the famous Barn Kelp. The area was lightly fished in those days and all species were abundant. It was especially good for kelp and sand bass, but we routinely collected barracuda, white seabass and yellowtail. Almost every trip we had one or more hookups on black seabass, seldom landing them as they invariably wrapped up in the thick weeds. We also found big halibut off Salt Creek, I remember. It was on the SUNSHINE that I made my all-time personal record catch of fifteen large white seabass.

Sam fished for King throughout the war. In 1946, Norm Hagen became a partner when he financed the new boat SPORTKING, and later bought King's interest entirely. Sam ran the new boat for years, moving to San Pedro and Santa Barbara as Norm's Landing concessions opened in those locations. He made friends with anglers at all the ports and became one of the most popular skippers on the South Coast.

Tiring of the moves away from home and family, Sam switched to San Clemente pier and a five year stint skippering the REEL FUN. From 1962 to 1974 Sam ran the private vessel DORSAL for Elmer Hehr, concentrating on broadbill swordfish and taking hundreds.

In recent years he has guided the fishing yacht BIG MIKE and we met again in San Diego where Sam had brought the boat for a bit of albacore fishing. It was a great pleasure to talk over old times and the changes that had taken place in the 44 years since we worked together.

Our conversation recalled boats, people and scenes associated with fishing out of the old Newport. We spoke of the vessels MUSIC, MAY B, SKIP-A-LOU, BLUE WATER, ZOOTSME II and many others. Our ebullient boss Darrell King, Bill Odette, skipper of VALENCIA III, Joe Dixon the bait man and Phil Tozer and his charter boats MOANA, CRYSTAL LEE and ANDELE—all came up. Incidentally, Phil was one of the few old timers still in the business as proprietor of Davey's Locker and the Balboa Pavilion.

Captain Cordeiro at the wheel.

Newport in the old days was as much a commercial as sport fishing center, home to hundreds of small craft scratching the sea for a living. Mackerel were scooped alive from the water and brought in by the ton to the three canneries: West Coast Packing, Gorby's, and Western Canners. They are all gone now. Most of the commercial fleet has vanished and even the real estate has changed drastically. A high rise building now stands on the site of King's Landing where I once slept on a boat and, among other tasks, had charge of night fishing on the bait receivers. It was good, too—lots of yellowfin croaker, small halibut and sea trout. Sam and I both detested the hard-starting hand-cranked diesel generator King had to light his parking lot and receivers.

Many of older readers will remember top-notch skipper Sam Cordeiro and the boats and people that flourished during the heyday of Newport Beach sportfishing when as many as sixty passenger boats were based at that port.

FRANK KIESSIG

In 1926 Frank Kiessig opened San Diego's first fishing barge, the IKE WALTON. In 1930 he tired of the logistical problems of barge operation and turned his attention to the developing mobile party boat fishery. To run regular trips to the Coronado Islands, the boat SAN ANTONIO was leased from the Schipper family. Fabulous catches ensured instant success and in 1932 Frank purchased and refitted the commercial vessel BETTY B. Renamed SPORTFISHER, she joined a growing fleet operating from floats

Brand new SPORTFISHER III at Terminal Island in 1938.

between the piers at the foot of Broadway: Mel Shears' MASCOT II, Guy Tadlock's YELLOWTAIL, Earl Menke's BIJOU, Nick Johns' AZTEC, and others.

Kiessig coupled imagination with energy and financial resources to introduce new concepts to the industry. According to his 1934 brochure, SPORTFISHER was 65 feet long with a 120 hp diesel engine, good cabin accommodations, cushion seats, a nice upper deck and a separate rest room for ladies. There was also a galley and card room, and a brochure claimed "No firearms allowed." Also, "No commercial fishermen allowed, and NO ONE is allowed to hog the stern." Competition spurred the introduction of the rotation system and the cleaning of the catch free of charge. San Diego boats were the first to offer these services.

In 1935 Frank met the challenge of Oakley Hall's new SEA ANGLER, first built-for-the-purpose sportboat, with SPORTFISHER II. The new boat, a 65-footer, was licensed for 75 passengers and could sleep 18. She was powered by a 150 hp Fairbanks Morse diesel with a Lister 5 kw auxiliary, and had a cruising range of 2,000 miles.

Kiessig pioneered long range trips when he sent the SPORTFISHER II to Cabo San Lucas in October 1936. She carried four skiffs equipped with swivel chairs and outboard motors. One of the anglers, Mike Wartnik, boated five marlin on his first morning out and was unable to lift his right arm for the rest of the trip. The twelve passengers on this first 14-day trip returned with 54 marlin and 23 sailfish packed in ice—a catch that caused a sensation in angling circles. In August 1937 skipper Tony Johansen began regular five and six day trips to Guadalupe Island, returning with big yellowtail, tuna and giant seabass. The largest yellow landed was reported to be 80 lbs and the biggest tuna 183 lbs. Frank called these excursions "Wanderlust Tours."

A new boat even better suited for extended cruises was SPORTFISHER III, built in 1938. She had bunks for 36 and a 3,000 mile range.

As the sportfishing business boomed a dependable supply of live bait became imperative. Prime "racehorse" sardines, six to eight inches long, were nearly always available to San Diego anglers. On the rare occasions when they were not, the grumbling was long and loud. Kiessig had constructed several experimental receivers to stow bait for his barge, but it was not until 1934 that the ultimate answer was found. After 15 different models had been tried, a design was adopted that is still in use today. The commercial boat ITALY was contracted to keep the ten receivers full and Dominic Sanfilippo became keeper of the sardines. The smaller bait fish were fed a daily ration of Cream of Wheat cereal and carefully tended until they reached six inches or more in length. Seasoned bait, healthy but used to confinement, was essential on the long range trips and receiver capacity was doubled to twenty boxes. Frank, always concerned about the bait supply, was aghast at the 1938 quota of 900,000 tons of sardines for reduction, but his objections to the Department of Fish & Game were of no avail.

Frank was something of a practical joker and the SPORTFISHER's galley was hung with neckties snipped from fishermen while they were busy battling yellowtail. Attached to the ties were cards with the victims' names. Inattentive anglers often found a bucket or a doll stuffed with sinkers attached to their lines. Black rings around the eyes would result when unsuspecting passengers were invited to look through binoculars with greased eyepieces. Such high jinks by the crews were common then. I saw Deck Captain Tex Miller unhook a man's bib overalls while he was fighting a fish and when a customer tried to go commercial with a handline, Tex tossed it overboard while the greedy one was getting a bait.

Entrepreneur Frank Kiessig (left) poses with marlin in front of his ticket office.

Mike Milas and friends pile their fish on deck. Mel Shears (back turned) wets a line. No seats or other accommodations for passengers are visible.

Progressive-minded Kiessig spent the early months of 1938 keeping an eye on the construction of the SPORTFISHER III at the Al Larsen yard on Terminal Island. Incorporating the lessons of experience, the new boat would sleep 36 passengers and have a 3,000 mile range. With a capacity of 75 tons, the vessel could be converted for commercial tuna fishing during winter months.

Failing health began to overtake Frank in 1938 and he finally passed away in July, 1939. According to his wishes, his ashes were scattered at sea south of Pt. Loma. The entire San Diego fleet formed a procession of boats paying their respects to one who had done much to further the sportfishing industry.

Frank's son Otto carried on the business until World War II halted operations. The SPORTFISHER fleet was rebuilt at war's end and merged with H & M in 1949 when the landings were moved to the Point Loma location. The last boats were sold off in 1952.

Displaying the catch on MASCOT 2 in 1929. Surplus fish were sold by the crew.

SENIOR SKIPPER: MEL SHEARS

The skipper emeritus of the entire California partyboat fleet was unquestionably Milford R. Shears, who was issued his 12th Coast Guard operator license in 1979. There are a few other real veteran captains still around—Ed McEwen, for example—but as far as I know Mel was the senior operator still working in 1984. His first license was obtained in 1924 and at age 76 Mel was still running boats. The oldest old-timer guided the half day boat DAILY DOUBLE from San Diego's Pt. Loma Association on a part-time basis. His vast experience gave him unequalled knowledge of local fishing areas which tells particularly when scratch conditions prevail, as in winter fishing for bull sand bass and shallow water rockfish. Every little rock pimple, weed patch or bit of wreckage can harbor its quota of fish and Mel knew them all.

Mel was born 5 February 1907 in Los Angeles but moved to San Diego while still an infant. His first memory of fishing was from his father's lap when about five years old, handlining from the old coaling wharf in San Diego Bay. There were some turbulent times in his young life and

Mel Shears, on right, as an H & M skipper.

the boy wound up in the Venice area relying on his own resources.

Shears began his fishing career when he found work at age 10 with Capt. T. J. Morris, the first operator of party fishing boats at Santa Monica. He worked on the salt bait boats URSULA and JOSIE M. and later on other Morris boats such as the PALISADES and FASHION. He was deckhand on the latter boat when she burned and sank on 9 June 1927. Young Milford slept in a back room of Frank Volke's bait house on the end of the Santa Monica pier. He learned to patch baitnets and do other odd jobs for Capt. Morris, while a kindly Mrs. Morris banked part of his wages for him.

In 1928 Mel purchased the MASCOT II, a vessel 63 feet long by 13 feet beam, powered with a 40 HP Frisco gas engine, and began one of the first party fishing ventures from San Diego. Live bait was obtained from commercial boats when possible but fishing with salt bait and trolling was also done. Fare was $2.50 local and $3.50 to the Coronado Islands. Departure time from Broadway Pier was 0630 and return was when sacks were full. Mel says he used to lure customers by hanging yellowtail and tuna to his rails while cruising close to the Pt. Loma barges.

Competing with Shears, Kiessig and Schipper in San Diego were Earl Menke with the BIJOU, Joe Bassinger with the AZTEC, Guy Tadlock with the YELLOWTAIL, Ed Johns with RADIO I and II, and Nick Johns with SHIRLEY ANN. All these businesses operated until abruptly ended by the coming of World War II.

In 1931, with the Depression in full swing, Shears was forced to give up the MASCOT II. She was bought by the H & M Company, operators of a fleet of water taxies. Mel went to work for Frank Kiessig, running the charter boat MORE FUN. For 14 trips in one season he landed 25 marlin and a broadbill. Al Thieler, a well-known angler and sporting goods dealer from Long Beach, got the 481-pound swordfish. Along with skippers Tony Johansen and Dean Hueck, Mel participated in the pioneering long range jaunts of the SPORTFISHER II.

When passenger trips were not scheduled, supplemental income was earned by commercial fishing, mostly for tuna and skipjack. One winter Mel wrapped 88 Calcutta rods for H & M to use as rental tackle. During World War II Shears operated water taxies and tugs for the Star and Crescent Co. at San Diego. After the hostilities he worked again for H & M, running the MASCOT III, which will be remembered by many of my older readers. The old tub was originally a schooner in the coastal trade, hauling turtles and onyx from San Quintin, but was fitted with two engines as a fishing boat. A long stint operating from Mission Bay was next.

Mel claimed he had retired six times, but kept answering the call of the sea. One look at him left little doubt that fishing, the Greatest Sport, contributes to man's longevity. Milford Shears passed on in July 1988 at the age of 81. The Oldest Skipper crown now passes to Eddie McEwan.

GUY SILVA, THE FISHING INVENTOR

It was in 1931 that I first saw the film "Tiger Shark," starring Edward G. Robinson and Richard Arlen. Fishing scenes made the general public aware for the first time of the exciting live bait and pole method of catching tuna. So stimulated was my own boyish imagination that I yearned for years afterward for the opportunity to participate in similar action.

The movie was shot aboard the clipper EMMA R. S., owned and operated by Captain Guy Silva. Warner Brothers executives conceived the idea after viewing a short subject about tuna fishing made aboard the boat. With a corny plot and poor production values, the film is now seen only on Turner Broadcasting's late-night TV show. The fishing sequences remain fascinating.

Silva was undoubtedly the most innovative of all the pioneer California commercial tuna fishermen. He is credited with inventing the steel fishing racks that were hinged outboard on the after bulwarks of the boats. Lifting heavy fish aboard with poles from outside the hull was much less awkward and dangerous than fishing from the deck and having the tuna fall onto legs and feet.

Actor Edward G. Robinson and Guy Silva during filming of "Tiger Shark" in 1931.

Guy Silva was born in St. Louis, Missouri, in 1890. Of Italian extraction, he was in no way related to the Portuguese Silvas later prominent in the tuna fleet. Arriving in San Diego in 1906, the teenager was immediately fascinated with the sea. A natural outdoorsman, he became an avid fisherman and hunter. In short order he had his first boat, the sloop RAMONA. Guy studied electrical engineering at the University of California at Berkeley and married in 1910. He acquired a 30-foot motor-sailer, VAGABOND, and ran charter trips and fished for the market. After service as an aviator in the World War, he was attracted to the booming canned tuna industry.

Already an experienced fisherman, Silva was among the first to pursue albacore for the newly-built canneries. VAGABOND was replaced with the 45-foot NACHI. Never reluctant to experiment with new techniques, he was one of the first to adopt the Japanese method of jackpole fishing for albacore.

As his fortunes grew with the expansion of the tuna industry, the talented and intelligent Silva was always at the cutting edge of new technology. In 1920 his new 65-foot boat ALICE was among the first to feature a diesel engine. In 1927 he upgraded to the 75-foot LOIS S., equipping her with the first ice-holding ammonia refrigeration machine.

EMMA R.S. on trial runs, 1929.

The fish hold was insulated with four-inch thick cork throughout. Value of the new cooling plant was proven when an entire load was landed in good shape after 31 days at sea, some fish being held for 26 days.

EMMA R. S., Silva's ultimate boat, was launched by San Diego Marine Construction Co. in 1928. She had a 95-foot flush-decked hull incorporating many of the owner's ideas, including a 3,000 mile range. The first diesel electric generator was installed to drive pumps and refrigeration. Notable was the slope-roofed deck tank designed to minimize destabilizing slosh while carrying five tons of bait. The tank was also insulated to provide extra fish storage. Guy's active mind generated continuous ideas for alterations and improvements during the life of the vessel.

He invented a type of magneto, or ignition system, for internal combustion engines, and he received patents for a number of electrical devices.

In 1929 a radio set, another first in the tuna fleet, was installed and immediately used to advantage in saving another boat, the LOIS S., from a busted trip. Silva sent a radiogram and parts to repair her disabled auxiliary were sent south on the departing clipper SAN JOAQUIN.

To better withstand rough seas a raised forward deck and enclosed bow were added to EMMA in 1930. RASCAL, A 17-foot speedboat modeled after the original CIGARETTE and capable of 30 m.p.h., was carried for recreational use by the 10-man crew.

Catching bait for tuna. Grey Silva in center.

The first attempt at aerial fish scouting was made in 1931 with a float plane to be carried atop the bait tank. The idea proved impractical for the size of the boat, but planes and helicopters were used in later years on a number of the larger tuna vessels.

The rich Galapagos Islands tuna banks were visited by EMMA R. S. in 1932, a 6,000-mile round trip that was usually considered outside the range of a 95-foot boat. Guy's son, Grey, who served as mate, navigator and radio operator from 1928 to 1941, rounded up some penguins and brought them home to be the first of their kind exhibited at the San Diego Zoo.

The longest fishing cruise on record was made in 1935 when the crankshafts of the auxiliary and main engines both broke. By disconnecting the broken part of the shaft and the attached piston, the boat was able to limp into Panama. Parts were ordered by radio and the smaller shaft was airmailed while the main was shipped by steamer. EMMA finally returned home after five months with 105 tons of tuna.

While his boat was in port undergoing repairs, Silva exercised his considerable diplomatic skill by negotiating with the Costa Rican government for bait-catching permits. As a result of his efforts, U.S. tunaboats were allowed to net bait in the Gulf of Nicoya after paying an annual fee of $125. It was an important benefit for the fishermen. Ongoing squabbles with the Mexicans over permit fees often restricted boats from baiting up at the traditional Magdalena and Banderas Bay grounds.

A legend was born when a giant basking shark once clung so closely to the side of EMMA R. S. that fishing was completely spoiled. The wary tuna, although in a biting mood, would not come within reach of the hooks. In a fit of frustration skipper Guy gripped the low bulwarks in both hands and vaulted over, stomping down with both feet on the shark's back! The monster took no apparent notice but in due course it swam away of its own accord.

The most revolutionary of Silva's inventions was a system for electrocuting outsize tuna. It usually took four or five men to bring giant tuna aboard and they were often reluctant to bite on the heavy gear and big hooks necessary to capture them. It occurred to Silva that by stunning the fish with electricity fewer men and lighter tackle could handle the catch. Guy worked on the scheme for several years, but LOIS S. was the first boat with sufficient voltage available to make a test. A 150-pound shark was his first victim, but it took further refinements and demonstrations to convince a wary crew that the rig was safe.

A metal ring fixed to the tip of a single 14-foot bamboo pole was connected to the positive side of a 120-volt direct current through an insulated wire. The negative side was grounded through the hook and steel leader in the water. When a tuna took the bait the circuit was closed and the fish shocked to immobility in 50 seconds. Two men, with an electrified pole and a gaff, could readily catch a 300-pound tuna that formerly took four men to handle. One load of fish taken with this gear averaged seven fish to the ton, with the largest weighing 328 pounds. The system was eventually discontinued when it proved usable only in calm seas.

A push-button controlled mechanical topping lift for fishing poles was perfected by Silva in 1948. An electrically-driven reel mounted atop the bait tank canopy held a quarter-inch line running to the tip of a standard tuna pole. When a fish struck, the fisherman would press a button taped to the pole and the high-speed reel would take the full weight of the fish and haul the line and tip of the pole up and back over the deck. At that point the reel reversed allowing the line to pay out. One man could land a fish of any size without undue exertion. The entire in-and-out cycle took about four seconds. On a trial run 11 tuna with a combined weight of nearly 1500 pounds were landed in a few minutes fishing. The system was not adaptable to rough seas when the roll of the boat pulled hooks out of the water. Using compressed air as a driver, Silva experimented with a similar rig as far back as 1922, but it proved unworkable.

After serving as an advisor to the navy on the employment of the tuna boats for war service, Guy resumed fishing when hostilities ceased. EMMA R. S., along with other tuna clippers, was used as a patrol craft. Cement was poured into the hold for ballast and Silva was never able to remove it completely. With the crew unable to reach and repair a leak due to the cement, the boat sank off Panama in 1950. Guy Silva retired from the sea and passed on in 1965. Always ready to assist fellow fishermen with aid and advice on mechanical or electrical problems, he was respected and admired throughout the fishing community.

ZANE GREY

For spending large sums of money in pursuit of a hobby I doubt anyone has matched Zane Grey. He made millions in a time when a dollar had twenty times its present worth and he spent a high proportion of his income on sportfishing. Although most famous for his western novels, his fishing books did much to generate worldwide interest in the sport. Grey and Charles Frederick Holder, founder of the Tuna Club, deserve equal credit for publicizing the great sea angling to be found off Southern California.

As a boy, I thrilled to his accounts of adventures beyond my wildest dreams. Now, I find his rather flamboyant style a little overdone, but there still is real pleasure in reading of the great pioneer's exploits with rod and reel.

The future novelist was born Pearl Grey in Zanesville, Ohio in 1872 and caught the fishing fever at an early age. Pearl trained as a dentist at the University of Pennsylvania and was a star baseball player. He opened an office in New York but hated dentistry and the name Pearl. Changing his name to Zane, after a distinguished ancestor, he tried writing. Success eluded him until *Riders of the Purple Sage* became a best seller. By 1925 he was making over half a million dollars a year on his western novels. Additional wealth poured in from the over 100 movies made from 50 of his works.

Guy Silva tried to ease the task of catching big tuna.

In January 1906 he honeymooned in California and caught a shark from the pier at the Hotel Del Coronado. It was his first taste of saltwater fishing. His wife Dolly later wrote, "This was the beginning of Grey's sea fishing. How mountainous it became!" He fished nearly every day and later spent a week at Catalina. Dolly's diary entry for the fifth of February: "Today I caught my big albacore."

Grey returned to Avalon in 1914 and summered there every year through 1927. It took him five years to catch a "button" tuna of over 100 pounds, but he made up for it by concentrating on marlin and swordfish. He considered himself the developer of and expert on broadbill fishing and eventually landed an impressive 23 of the species.

He was one of the first to fish for giant bluefin tuna in Nova Scotia. His 758-pound tuna was a record in 1924. While there he bought a big schooner and had her converted, at great expense, to a cruising yacht equipped with fishing launches. In 1925 he made an exploratory trip from Panama to Cabo San Lucas, including the Galapagos and Cocos Islands. He tested waters never before fished by sportsmen.

Tales of Fishing Virgin Seas, the story of that cruise, was my favorite of Zane Grey's books. Perhaps it was because his teenage son Romer figured prominently in the story, and I was fourteen when I first read the book. He also dealt with some Pacific Ocean fish other than big game swordfish and tuna.

Grey and his party visited the Cocos, Perlas, and Galapagos islands, Zihuatanejo and the Cape, and found fabulous fishing everywhere. Most of these spots had never been trolled over with a rod and reel.

Grey himself was primarily interested in swordfish and billfish, but none were found until the ship reached the Mexican coast. It is too bad he didn't find the black marlin and sailfish of the Gulf of Panama, but apparently they fished the wrong area at the wrong time. Off Zihuatanejo he found sailfish and marvelled at their size compared to the Atlantic variety. There he lost a black marlin at gaff and boated a 135-pound sailfish. Zane's brother R. C. landed three sailfish in one day.

Romer and his pal Johnny were content with the smaller varieties abundant everywhere. They caught wahoo, dol-

Record marlin and broadbill were prime targets for Zane Grey. "Luke Tailwalker," from a painting by the author.

phin, tuna, roosterfish, crevalle, runners, snappers, groupers and other exotics in profusion.

"For catching fish and battling the monsters of tropic seas we had every kind of tackle that money could buy and ingenuity devise," wrote Grey. Murphy and Leonard rods of hickory and split bamboo were fitted with Vom Hofe and Coxe reels. Grey complained of the miles of expensive linen line and hundreds of lures that were lost to sharks and unknown monster fish. Whole and strip baits, Wilson spoons, feather jigs, Tarporenos and "solid metal Catalina minnows" were trolled. Tarporenos were larger copies of a popular wooden bass plug manufactured by the South Bend Bait Co. Shaped like a cigar with a scooped-out head, it had a violently erratic motion when drawn through the water. Grey found it a great attractor but not rugged enough for big fish. He drug it on a short line, minus hooks, as a teaser for billfish. You don't see much of that these days, but Grey used teasers regularly.

At Cabo San Lucas the catch was mostly large yellowfin tuna close to shore. Grey caught seven in one day ranging from 135 to 215 pounds. He also boated a record fish of 318 pounds and young Romer took one of 184 pounds.

In spite of his vast fishing experience, Grey misidentified many of the fish they caught. It is understandable as scientific information on the exotics was sparse at the time. A 65-pound broomtail grouper hooked by Romer was labelled a "rock bass." The tuna were called "Allisons" and a large blue marlin taken by commercials was thought to be a black. The clear photos in the Virgin Seas book make correct hindsight identification easy.

Grey became obsessed with exploring unknown waters. "Nothing thrilled me so much as virgin fishing," he wrote. In 1926, at the invitation of the New Zealand government, he introduced American methods and tackle to those distant islands. In addition to numerous marlin and makos, he boated a world record yellowtail of 111 pounds.

Grey was admittedly somewhat gullible and wrote, "A fisherman will believe anything." He was convinced of the existence of sea serpents and more than once wrote yearningly of huge 25-foot sailfish rumored to lurk in the Indian Ocean. On a visit to Tahiti he heard native tales of underbill swordfish, 10-foot barracuda and 50-foot sharks, and swallowed them all. We now know that these creatures were in the same fantasy realm as Conan Doyle's "giant rat of Sumatra."

After exploring Tahitian waters in his yacht in 1928, he mounted a major shore-based expedition to the area in 1929. It is unlikely that such profligate spending in pursuit of gamefish has ever been equalled. Eight portable bungalows and three custom built launches were shipped to the remote islands by steamer. Extra thousands were spent on custom tackle such as Murphy hickory rods, Kovalovsky reels and special lines. All expenses were paid for a large retinue of fishing buddies, guides, cameramen, secretaries and camp staff.

Grey did not spare himself extreme physical hardship while chasing his dream. He once drug a big bonito bait "heavy as a log" on a hand-held rod for nine hours and trolled a 20-pound tuna for four hours before turning over the rod. His boats were not equipped with outriggers or rod holders.

He liked the feel of the tropical sun on his bare shoulders, but seriously overexposed himself. "I had a couple of good long stares into the sun, which violet ray treatment I find wonderfully beneficial. I do not wear dark glasses anymore to protect my eyes from the glare," he wrote. It is no wonder that after long days trolling he complained of headaches, fatigue and the "blind staggers."

Compared to his brother R. C. and his fishing pal Capt. Mitchell, Grey was an unlucky fisherman, but his perseverance and determination were unsurpassed. He trolled 83 days without a catch before boating a 464-pound marlin. His tenacity was finally rewarded when he landed a 1,040-pound Tahitian blue marlin. It was the first thousand-pounder ever landed on rod and reel. In Australia another record was set with a 1,036-pound tiger shark.

Grey's somewhat egocentric ways made him controversial and unpopular with some of his fellow anglers. Effusive letters about his fishing exploits aroused magazine editor Robert H. Davis to reply that: "If you went out with a mosquito net to catch a mess of minnows your story would read like Roman gladiators seining the Tigris for whales....You say 'the hard, diving fight of a tuna liberates the brute instinct in a man.' Well, Zane, it also liberates the qualities of a liar!" Stung by such comments, Grey attributed them to jealousy. Be that as it may, Zane Grey was a true pioneer of big game fishing and his books generated worldwide interest in the sport. His tales thrilled me as a youngster and are still fun to read.

Zane Grey died of heart failure at his home in Altadena on October 23, 1939. He had been planning yet another Australian adventure.

SCHIPPER AND SONS

Another tale of pioneer sportfishing enterprise began in 1929 when a family of Great Lakes commercial fishermen migrated to San Diego from Fairport,

Michigan. Intending to ply their trade in Pacific waters, they purchased the SANANTONIO, a typical 50-foot market boat powered by a three-cylinder Union gasoline engine.

Lacking experience in ocean fishing, Michael Schipper and his four sons, Leonard, Louis, Maurice and Fred, were soon in financial difficulty. A friend, Ed Heverline, took Michael on a trip aboard the MASCOT No.2. Schipper returned from the cruise intrigued by the sportfishing potential just beginning to unfold in San Diego.

It so happened that Frank Kiessig wanted to try the party boat business at this time. He already had a landing location and a successful fishing operation with his famous barge IKE WALTON, launched in 1926. Kiessig leased the SAN ANTONIO for a year, the profits to be split 50-50 with the Schippers. The boat was easily converted for sportfishing by the addition of a stout wooden liferail and a box to contain enough life jackets for the 35 passengers allowed by the Coast Guard.

The joint venture was immediately successful. In 1931, under the tutelage of veteran San Diego hand Dean Hueck, the Schippers went into business for themselves. Fishing was great and on August 9th of that year Hueck reported a catch of 132 yellowtail for 25 anglers and a marlin hooked and lost. The business prospered in spite of Depression hard times and in 1935 a diesel engine was installed in the TONY, the Schippers affectionate nickname for their boat. The above deck structure was also altered as the pilot house was shifted forward. The boat also sported a new coat of white paint in place of the old green color scheme. In 1936, after Michael passed on, Leonard took over direction of the business, skippering the boat as Louis and Maurice handled deck duties and Fred manned the tiny galley. World War II halted San Diego sportfishing and the navy took over the TONY as a tender for training divers. When the boat was returned after the war she was sold to Mexican buyers and the Schippers were never again active in sportfishing. Leonard returned to commercial fishing and worked in big tuna clippers, becoming chief engineer of the HEROIC until he retired in 1957.

In 1988 it was my great good fortune to locate and interview Leonard Schipper. He very kindly allowed me to borrow his collection of old photo negatives from which I obtained some 150 prints of fishing activities on the SAN ANTONIO. They recall happy memories of riding with the firm of Schipper & Sons, especially the trip in September 1936 when I captured four yellowfin tuna, three skipjack and five yellowtail at the Coronado Islands.

Herewith is a sampling from the collections chosen for the flavor and feeling of live bait sportfishing as it was 60 years ago.

Action on the TONY. Gent in golfing knickers (center) looks for a spot at the rail.

Green-painted SAN ANTONIO in 1931.

SAN ANTONIO after 1935 alterations.

Michael handlines one (center) as unconcerned anglers play fish and re-rig.

Satisfied customer poses with his catch. Michael Schipper on the right.

Michael Schipper chums as Maurice stands by with gaff. Formally dressed gent at lower right prepares to cast. Rifle by hatch was used to shoot marauding sea lions.

Handlining and crew fishing was not unusual on sportboats 60 years ago.

Ouch! Long butt of Eastern-style surf rod makes playing heavy fish awkward and dangerous.

Lady angler struggles with finny fighter near Pukey Point on North Coronado. Note bulging sacks of yellows.

Angler in trouble. The outcome is in doubt.

This kind of fun can be painful.

"Take a Strain," from a painting by the author. Classic 4-pole tuna fishing.

Lampara boats wait to unload sardines at Fish Harbor canneries, 1919. These boats would pursue albacore in season.

Chapter 13
BYCATCH: ODDS AND ENDS

MAKE-DO FISHING

Long, long ago, in an ocean far, far away, the warlords decreed that I should sojourn for a time on a coral dot called Eniwetok Atoll. The lagoon there swarmed with fish, large and small, in all the profuse variety of tropic seas. The sailors and marines occupying the island, busy with the war, rarely found time to try their luck. When they did fish, they were usually hampered by limited skill or inadequate tackle. Faced with months of arduous duty and few recreational facilities, those of us who were dedicated anglers persisted in our search for ways and means to reduce the fish population.

Reposing in the depths of my seabag, along with a bit of leader wire, a few hooks and a Dodger jig, was an old Penn Long Beach reel filled with 12-thread line. Stored there also were a few ring guides and a rod tip. On a previous deployment to the South Pacific, I had seen numerous stands of bamboo on the islands and expected no difficulty in finding one usable as a fishing rod.

Except for a few coconut stumps and pandanus bushes, no vegetation of any kind remained on shell-blasted Eniwetok. There was absolutely nothing suitable for a fishing rod. I made do with a pair of pup-tent poles—wooden dowels about two feet long, joined by a metal sleeve. The pole had no spring and no taper. One end was whittled down to fit the tip-top, friction tape fastened the guides and hose clamps secured the reel.

Next, some kind of boat was needed to get out where the big ones lived. As all the Navy small craft were otherwise occupied, I had to build my own small ark. Two wide planks of rough dunnage served for sides and sawn boxwood made bottom planks and thwarts. Plywood blades fastened to 2 x 4 shafts made a pair of clumsy oars. Rope grommets secured them to tent peg hole pins. The crude vessel was caulked with tar-like gunk used by the SeaBees for waterproofing Quonset huts. After a few weeks of intermittent labor, I had a punt of sorts. It was an odd, square-ended contraption and awkward to handle—but it floated!

One hot afternoon, after a jeering send-off from skeptical comrades, I finally pushed off in my cranky crate. Paddling a few hundred yards, I reached a spot in the lagoon where a great coral head reared up from the bottom. My

Building the punt

anchor, the breechblock of a Japanese field gun, was carefully lowered and my adventure began.

On my second cast with the Dodger I let the lure sink deep before starting the retrieve. I could see it far down, flashing as it moved up past the pillar of coral. Suddenly, two dark forms darted from the green gloom of a rocky cave. An arm-jolting strike recalled fishing's greatest thrill.

After several strong, surging runs I gained control and pumped the fish toward the boat. At last, a sizeable grouper of twenty pounds or so, all red-brown with blue spots, rolled to the surface alongside. As I slipped my hand into his gills to lift him aboard another much larger fish was seen following my captive.

Quickly boating my catch I cast again and, sure enough, was rewarded with another strike more vicious than the first. My makeshift rod of stiff wood, totally unsuited for real fishing, cracked ominously. To ease the excessive tension I backed off the drag. This mistake gave the fish sufficient advantage to succeed in a dash for the coral. In a matter of seconds the line frayed and parted. So, once again, "the big one got away." I was not too disheartened, for I had taken one good fish and that was enough to convince the skeptics.

My fishing success increased dramatically when, not long after that first venture, I was able to buy a real split bamboo rod from a bomber crewman on his way back to the U.S. Also acquired was a patched-up aviator's rubber life raft, a great improvement over my clumsy punt. In it I could paddle to where ranks of sectional causeway barges were moored. Sheltering beneath them were schools of scad, a sort of jack mackerel, and they could be chummed with canned peas until they were thick enough to snag.

I finally pushed off in my cranky crate.

A live scad on a flyline drew immediate attention from big crevally jacks, barracuda or ferocious dogtooth tuna *(Gymnosarda unicolor).* The latter fish grow to over 150 pounds, but the ones I caught in the lagoon were generally under 30 pounds. They resemble large, stripeless bonito with oversize heads and huge mouths armed with rows of long teeth. They are strong fighters and will attack prey nearly as large as themselves.

The author in 1946 captured barracuda and tuna at Guam.

During the Solomon Islands campaign my aircraft carrier anchored between sorties at the small port of Vila on Efate Island in the New Hebrides group. As a way to escape the confines of the ship for a few hours each day, I volunteered for boat coxswain duty. An LCVP was drawn from the port boat pool and with it I prowled the harbor on various errands. Plenty of fish were showing in the calm waters of the anchorage and I yearned to catch a few. In the early morning I would carry the garbage cans from the ship to a dump on the beach. For the opportunity to scavenge the tins and scraps of discarded clothing, friendly Melanesian natives would empty and clean the cans. Food scraps in the water chummed up hordes of colorful tropic fish species and I caught many while waiting at the dump. My tackle was a small hook on a piece of string tied to the end of a

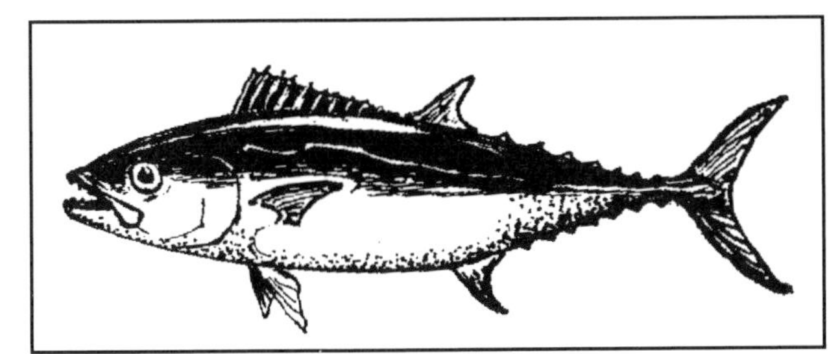

Dogtooth tuna

boathook. It was interesting, but not very sporting.

Trolling while on my daily cruises seemed the logical way to catch gamefish. Trouble was, no gear was available. I had picked up a few hooks at a shop in Vila, but had nothing else. It was time to improvise. Some stainless wire scrounged from the aviation mechanics served for leaders. A hank of the cotton "white line" cord used by the deck force for decorative work made a stout handline. Lures were still lacking.

Experiments with various materials followed. Feathers plucked from a torn pillow proved too short for jig making and strips of rag were unproductive. Large numbers of navy issue rubber condoms reposed in personal lockers awaiting the first liberty port. It occurred to me that if I cut the tip from a condom and sliced the tube into strips, it would simulate the legs of a squid. Short pieces of broom handle were turned down in the ship's carpenter shop to resemble the bullet shape of feather jig heads. A hole was drilled longitudinally and red and white paint applied. Next, two condoms with their rear halves trimmed to resemble squid legs were bound to each wooden head with sail twine. Strung on a wire leader they were very similar to albacore trolling jigs in use today.

Unless high ranking officers were aboard, the makeshift condom jigs were trolled on all my boat trips around the anchorage. Not a lot of fish were taken in the harbor waters but, to my great satisfaction, I did manage a few. Crevally jacks, pargos, sierras, and a small dog tooth tuna snapped at the rubber jigs. They were not rugged and a few strikes were enough to shred them. The fish were returned to the water or donated to grateful natives.

Other lures were fashioned from strips of tin cut from five-gallon coffee cans. Filed, hammered and drilled, they came to resemble crude fishing spoons. By the time I had made a reasonably good one, our respite in Vila ended and no opportunities for field testing were forthcoming.

In later years I took yellowfin tuna, barracuda and milkfish at Guam and giant barracuda at the former Japanese island fortress Truk. Always I had the satisfaction of knowing that the basic fishing skills I had learned on the California coast could be successfully applied anywhere.

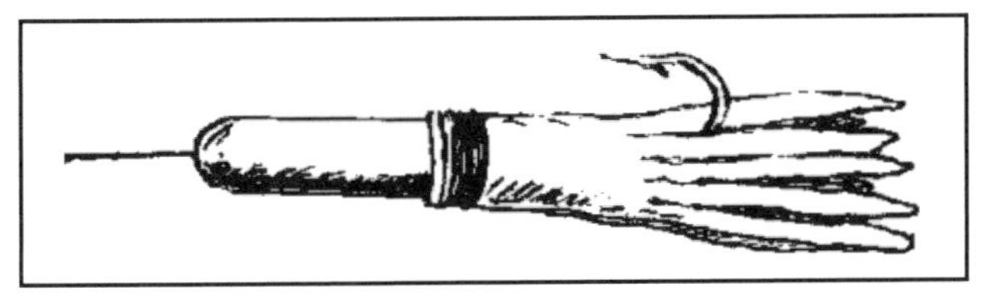

The condom jig.

FISHING FASHIONS

One of the favorites in my collection of old fishing photos appears in C. F. Holder's "The Channel Islands of California." It shows a very large black seabass of 416 pounds taken by Mrs. A. W. Barrett in 1906. The locale is Catalina and the pose is typical. Staring grimly at the camera, the doughty lady angler clutches her wooden rod and knuckle-buster reel. Especially remarkable is the clothing worn by the fisherwoman. For any kind of outdoor activity, let alone big game fishing, it is the most wildly inappropriate costume imaginable. Covering her from head to toe is a heavy black dress with high choker collar, long sleeves and a corseted, pinched-in waist. The gown obviously hides a thick layer of undergarments. A necklace, pin and wide-

Mrs. Barrett's 1906 catch.

brimmed hat top off the ensemble. Gaining sufficient breath and freedom of movement for the exertion required to land such a giant fish must have been nearly impossible.

Only the very well-off could afford charter fishing in those days. Being for the most part prim and conservative in their outlook, they adhered to a very formal dress code at all times, even at play. Given the heavy and constricting clothing they thought it necessary to wear, it is no wonder that few women participated in sportfishing.

The boatman, or gaffer as Holder always called him, wore more practical garb, including items of naval uniform

In spite of his formal dress, this angler scored a 29-lb. yellowtail on the barge PT. LOMA , 1928.

such as a white jumper and beribboned flat hat. The trio—lady, fish and gaffer—make a quaint, not to say bizarre, tableau that epitomizes the sort of handicaps those pioneer big game fishermen (and women) overcame. Not only was their tackle crude, they hampered themselves with clothing that by today's standards would equate to straitjackets. Sometimes it was downright dangerous.

Holder himself recounts the occasion when his boat capsized as a large tuna was gaffed and he went overboard clad in a corduroy hunting suit, canvas leggings and heavy shoes. He managed to swim to a nearby launch but could not climb aboard due to the weight of the waterlogged garments! It took considerable effort by several men to drag him to safety.

Other photos from the early days show the anglers nearly always wearing suit, tie and felt hat, as if dressed for business appointments. This mode was still seen on boats right up until World War II, although by that time clothing was generally less formal. With the advent of fishing barges and open party boats in the 'twenties, more blue-collar types took up sportfishing and a trend toward casual wear was underway. Many woolen olive drab army surplus items were visible, favored by sport and commercial alike. Overalls, dungarees and all kinds of working clothes were worn. About this time a fad developed among more affluent big game fishermen for baggy "plus-four" golfing knickers. Lady anglers began to appear in the loose slacks made popular by certain movie stars.

Hip length rubber boots were worn by all deckhands and commercial fishermen. Knee high leather lace-up "hiking boots" and wool breeches were considered appropriate wear for fishing by men and women alike.

The felt fedora, the Panama straw and the soft cloth cap were usual headgear, but boat crews usually wore the traditional hardbilled seaman's cap. Known as a "Lundberg Stetson," a white linen cap was the style for commercial fishermen in the 1930s. The "Florida cap" with an extra long bill made its California debut after the war. After losing several overboard I gave up on them. The awkward long bill frequently got in the way. Pole fishing tunamen found hard plastic helmet liners useful protection from flying hooks. In the purse-seine fleet, the liners have been supplanted by industrial hard hats. About the only other head cover worn is the light weight baseball-type cap.

Anything goes these days. Shorty boots and sleeveless vests seem to be the current vogue among those anglers who want to be thought of as semipro and salty. Last but not least, modern fishing ladies in their shorts, tight designer jeans and bikinis are a decorative addition to an already pleasant scene.

Breaches and hiking boots were considered appropriate for any kind of outdoor activity, including fishing.

OLD FISHING MAGAZINES

Outdoor Life, *Field & Stream*, *Sports Afield* and similar magazines enjoyed wide circulation sixty years ago. It was my custom then to eagerly peruse every issue of those pubs in search of more fishing knowledge. It amazed and frustrated me that our local salt water angling was almost completely ignored by the old Eastern-oriented magazines. An article on big game marlin or tuna occasionally found its way into print, but articles about California live bait and inshore fishing were nonexistent. Atlantic ocean activity got plenty of ink but we were left out. This began to change slightly at the end of World War II when J. Charles Davis II became Pacific editor of *Sports Afield*. The surviving magazines now report on West Coast fishing in every issue.

In their ads a multitude of tackle companies offered catalogs free or at a nominal price. As a teenager I collected them all and I regret their loss in a storeroom fire. They would be invaluable for research and worth a small fortune to collectors.

The Depression prices of the goods tendered and the magazines themselves are interesting. An issue of 118 pages of *Outdoor Life* sold for 15 cents in 1937. *Field & Stream* was 25 cents then, but now carries a tenfold price increase. The advertised cost of a Pfluger "Ohio" reel in 1934 was $6.50. An "Ohio" was my first star-drag reel, but in 1935 I had to peddle a lot of fish to accumulate even that modest sum. Pflueger also listed a knuckle-buster reel with free spool, the "Golden West," for $3.50. Ocean City had their similar "Brigantine" at $4, but their star-drag "Bay City" matched the "Ohio" price.

Big game fishermen could still find advertisements for the classic reels of Edward Vom Hofe and Pflueger's "Atlapac" selling for $65 to $100. In 1947 the Dumond reel in sizes 4-0 to 12-0 was touted, but it apparently never caught on in spite of claims that it would never freeze or strip gears.

Many of the advertisers specialized primarily in fresh water tackle, but some produced a few salt water items. Most of the brands, very well known then, are long since defunct. Some of the old familiar firms include: Arbogast, Ashaway, Creek Chub, Gladding, Heddon, Hildebrandt, Horrocks-Ibbotsen, Montague and Shakespeare, to name but a few. The Al Wilson Co. of San Francisco was still selling its famous spoons for 25 cents to 65 cents each in 1937. If one was looking for a rod, the South Bend Bait Co. had a surf stick of split bamboo complete with "spring butt" of hickory for $12, and a 6-foot 9-inch boat rod with over and under guides for $21. Most interesting were the twelve new salt water rods offered by Gephart Mfg Co. in 1937. Of tubular steel, a light tackle rig had a 14-inch butt, a five-foot tip, weighed six ounces and sold for $15. Ten years later another metal rod was on the market. Warren Products of Los Angeles advertised beryllium-copper alloy rods obtainable in lengths to 8½ feet. Their high cost of $43 to $75 in 1947 ruled out wide popularity, but I saw a number of them in use in the days before fiberglass took over.

1934 ad for Pflueger reels.

Apart from the old ads the most interesting feature of the magazines for me was their extensive use of art work. The full-color covers and about three fourths of the articles inside were illustrated by the recognized wildlife artists of the day. Covers dealing with salt water fishing featured mostly sailfish, tarpon, striped bass and channel bass in the surf. Artist Lynn Bogue Hunt drew many of these assignments and his works became favorites of mine. Other prominent illustrators appearing regularly in outdoor publications were Herman Rountree, Harold Titus, William Schaldack, Fred Everett and Howard Hastings. *Field & Stream* announced for sale the original cover paintings, mostly oils 18" x 24", but didn't quote a price in their ads. Anyone who bought one of those pieces in the '30s can be sure it has appreciated substantially in value over the years.

DERBY DAYS

San Diego's famous Yellowtail Derby, sponsored by the Junior Chamber of Commerce to promote tourism in San Diego, reached a peak of popularity in the 'fifties. In 1955 there were two Derby Days, one each in June and September, with qualifying periods preceding. A running list of the largest fish weighed in during the periods was narrowed down to the top 400. Qualified anglers were allowed to fish on Derby Day for the jackpot prizes of a new car, house trailer, outboard motor and other goodies. To keep interest at a high pitch additional prizes were awarded for the largest fish taken each week of the qualifying periods.

The summer started off well when I made it into the first Derby with a 25 pound bluefin tuna, but I failed to make a prize catch in the fish-off.

In July I scored a 27-pound, 8-ounce albacore on Bill Poole's old gray POLARIS, winning a jackpot, weekly first prize and a spot in the fish-off. The rod I won, a Silaflex SP105R2, at that time a Cadillac of fish poles, was most welcome. Until then I was still using my trusty old Calcutta bamboo stick. A Langley Spinator reel filled with line was also included, but it never got much use as I dislike spinning reels for heavy duty fishing. It was excellent for surf casting, though.

Derby Day, September 24, I was assigned to Chuck Chamberlain's OLDE IRONSIDES. Fishing was better than in the June Derby and all boats involved bagged a few yellows. I managed three, the largest 21 lb, 2 oz. Radio chatter on the homeward passage seemed to suggest that I had landed the big one, worth a Buick convertible. At the official weigh-in my fish was beaten by an ounce. I had to settle for second prize, a house trailer that I later converted to cash. All in all, it was a pretty good year for prizes and profits from fishing, but it would have been an enjoyable, fun-filled experience without prizes. They were just extra icing on the cake.

The Derby was born out of a 1936 scheme by the sport-fishing industry, local clubs and San Diego merchants. Originally called the Ocean Fishing Derby, it began in April and wound up with a ten-day fish-off from August 29 to September 7. Weekly prizes were also awarded. Anyone catching a yellowtail or tuna over 10 pounds was eligible if an entry ticket was obtained from his boat skipper. Marlin and broadbill also qualified.

Fishing was excellent in '36 and the competition started off with a bang when Fred Sutton of Long Beach took a 35 lb, 1 oz. yellow the first week. Mrs. J. Charles Davis, mother of writer Charlie, bagged nine yellowtail on the same trip. The big winner in the fish-off was L. O. Wetzell who sacked a 27 lb, 12 oz. yellow to take the grand prize, a Ford Tudor sedan "worth $800," a princely sum in the Depression era. M. R. Goree won second place with a 28 lb, 5 oz. yellowfin tuna which entitled him to a $150 fishing outfit. Due to administrative hassles, the derby of 1936 was a one-shot. Contests were not resumed until the Chamber of Commerce took over.

The decline in consistently good catches at the Coronado Islands led to the demise of the Yellowtail Derby. In any case, the contest was no longer needed as a tourist draw. In season, albacore and tuna are now more often the primary targets of the San Diego fleet.

CURIOUS FISHING FACTS

The last one hundred years have seen vast fluctuations in the abundance of certain species in our coastal fisheries. The decrease in availability of fish in general is probably due to overfishing and pollution of nearshore waters. However, not all the blame can be cast on human carelessness. There is strong evidence that cycles due to changing hydrographic conditions and other natural causes have an even greater influence on the lives of our finny favorites.

Over 71 percent of the total 1889 commercial catch of white seabass was landed in San Francisco and there was a flourishing gill net fishery for them in Monterey Bay.

From 1870 to 1890 the Monterey Spanish mackerel (*Scomberomorus concolor*) appeared in the bay each fall in sufficient numbers to become commercially important. This warm water fish is very similar to the sierra familiar to Baja anglers, but without the gold spots on the sides. The Monterey mackerel suddenly and completely disappeared for 40 years. Only six specimens were recorded in southern California until 1947. The fish is now caught occasionally in the Gulf, but is far less common than the sierra.

What happened to cause the disappearance of the seabass and Monterey mackerel? No water temperature records

Sablefish, or black cod.

were kept at the time but the evidence suggests that there was a prolonged El Nino extending the range of some species far to the north. We know from our own recent experience that even a short-duration effect can cause a drastic shift in fish populations.

The erratic behavior of our esteemed albacore is well known. After years of superabundance that formed the basic resource for the beginning of the canned tuna industry, albacore failed to appear in coastal waters in 1926 and except for short flurries were scarce until the 1940s. There has been another drought since 1985, but hopefully the runs will rebuild. Elimination of high seas driftnetting, will surely help.

Monterey was the site of another strange fish story in 1947. For the first time in history a huge swarm of sablefish appeared in the bay and were caught by the thousands from the municipal pier. For two weeks, from July 11th to the 26th, the 12 to 20-inch fish were taken on a variety of tackle. Men, women and children stood shoulder to shoulder hauling in their catch as fast as their lines could be cast. Each day the pier was jammed with crowds of from 2,000 to 5,000 fishermen and spectators, some having driven as far as 200 miles. The run ended as abruptly as it began and it was estimated by the Fish & Game that over 110 tons of the juvenile sablefish had been landed.

South Coast anglers rarely encounter sablefish, also known as black cod. They are usually found only at great depths, 1,000 feet or more, over mud bottoms. Rock cod fishermen sometimes make an incidental catch. In northern waters sablefish grow to four feet in length and are the object of intense commercial fishing with longlines and traps.

Broomtail groupers and cabrillas, species common to the lower reaches of Baja California, were once taken off the rocky areas of La Jolla. Some fishermen believe that the big basses were introduced as small fry dumped from the bait tanks of returning tuna clippers. Commercial live bait tuna fishing is now a thing of the past, but perhaps it is only coincidence that there are no more groupers at La Jolla.

There has been speculation that other semitropical species were inadvertently transported by the same means. It is

Monterey Spanish mackerel.

possible that a few may have come that way, but migration on warm currents is considered more likely. The highly touted bonefish, favorite of Florida anglers, and the bobo or threadfin, have both been taken on occasion in local waters.

Forty years ago there was a great run of large jack mackerel, to three pounds, along the Orange County coast and large numbers were sacked on sport boats. Smaller ones, usually called Spanish mackerel, are frequently snagged for yellowtail and tuna bait, but no similar run of the giants has been seen since.

Olive rockfish, sometimes called johnny bass, were so thick in the Point Loma kelp beds in the late sixties that it was difficult to keep them off the bait long enough to catch kelp bass. They were plentiful until about 1975 but their numbers have since dwindled until they are now relatively scarce. Where did they go?

It is clear that life in the sea moves through cycles of scarcity and abundance for reasons we can only imagine.

SEINERS AND SARDINES

Purse seining was perceived as the major threat to sport fishing in the Old Days. Gillnetting was known to be deleterious, but seining could, and did, wipe out whole schools of fish in one set. After slaughtering thousands of tons of white seabass, yellowtail and barracuda, seiners were gradually restricted in their take of these fish. Tuna, bonito, mackerel and above all, sardines remained their authorized prey. Catches of sardines grew to astronomical proportions and, coupled with a few poor spawning seasons, resulted in near extinction of the species.

The West Coast commercial sardine fishery began during the first world war and in 1918 the catch exceeded 150 million pounds. By 1920 it had become overwhelming in importance. Sardines made up about 85 percent of total fish of all kinds taken. Maximum decimation of the resource was attained in 1936 when a billion and a half pounds were strained from the sea. There followed an inevitable leveling off until 1945, after which came a very rapid decline.

In the early days they were incredibly abundant and easily caught in the newly-introduced Italian lampara roundhaul nets. The nets were pulled by hand and the fish were carried on deck and contained by side boards. The San Pedro launches were mostly of the type known as albacore chasers 40 to 55 feet in length manned by immigrant Japanese. The fish ranged in size from pinheads through "quarters" and "halves" to 14-inch "bohunks." The larger sizes made up the bulk of the catch.

The misuse of the sardine resource is a true ecological horror story. Millions of pounds were manufactured into poultry feed and fertilizer. In the first four months of 1919, 15,630,067 pounds of sardines were processed by reduction plants. In spite of the superabundance of sardines, over 7,000 tons of other fish were also fed to the plants, including 58,995 pounds of barracuda, 15,254 pounds of rockfish and 4,400 pounds of halibut. Up to June first, over 32,000,000 pounds of sardines were pulverized in reduction plants.

Bin boards formed pilot house access holes on these overloaded boats.

So huge was the catch of sardines that by the first part of May, the reduction plants could not handle all the fish brought in. Fishermen continued to bring in full loads of up to 26 tons per boat without regard to the 1,200 ton daily capacity of the San Pedro plants. Unfit even for reduction, in one day 185 tons of rotten fish were dumped at sea by order of the city health department.

In spite of some hand-wringing by a few Fish & Game biologists and protests from sportfishing interests, little was done to curb the massacre.

Large purse seine boats originally concentrated on other species, such as tuna, bonito, mackerel and the three so-called "whitefish" which in those days meant barracuda, yellowtail and white seabass. It was 1941 before roundhaul seining of the latter species was prohibited, although no restriction was placed on fish caught south of the border. Gillnetting remained legal until the present.

In 1925 purse seiners began to ship smaller-mesh nets and enter the sardine fishery. Their size, seaworthiness, deep holds, cruising range and mechanically aided net-handling enabled them to quickly dominate the fishery. The seines were about 200-250 fathoms long by 20-30 fathoms deep with a mesh size of one or 1¼ inches. Webbing was usually tarred. A series of steel rings slung from bridles on the lead-

Typical purse seiner of the 'thirties.

At Catalina a beach seine catches sardines for bait, 1905.

line were bunched, or pursed, with a cable hauled by a deck reel. The bottom of the net was thus closed, preventing the escape of any surrounded fish. The net was pulled by power winch and the catch brailed into the boat's hold by a huge scoop suspended from a boom.

The most productive fishing was at night during the dark of the moon. Restless movements of the schooled sardines would make a phosphorescent "fireball" easy to spot by seiner mastmen.

Monterey's famous Cannery Row was founded to process the sardines once swarming in the bay. Other major canneries were at San Pedro's Fish Harbor, located on Terminal Island. Lesser processing centers operated in San Diego and Newport Beach. The southern canneries also processed tuna and mackerel for food, but Monterey plants were entirely dependent on sardines. The supply of fish seemed inexhaustible and ever-increasing tonnages were taken. By 1935 the catch had climbed to 230,000 tons and that was exceeded during the war years. In 1945 Monterey had 20 reduction plants and 19 canneries supplied by over 100 boats.

The catch for 1946 was 100,000 tons less than the previous year and the decline continued until 1950, the last profitable season. By 1952 Cannery Row was finished. The sardines were gone.

Up until their disappearance in the 1950s, sardines were considered to be the "candy bait" for all sportfish. Squid came to the fore only after the sardines were defunct.

The closing of California's fish canneries in recent years has meant a drastic reduction in the purse seine fleet and a resurgence in the biomass of sardines. During the entire spring and summer of 1992, sardines were almost the only bait available for sportfishing on the South Coast. Warmer than average sea temperatures drove anchovy schools away, but fortunately a rebounding sardine population furnished ample supplies of live bait.

VIGNETTES

In my lifetime accumulation of fishing memories there are incidents that are especially vivid. Some, such as my shark encounters and three-pole tuna thrills, have been related. A sampling of others herewith:

After a couple hours of trolling across a bumpy sea one windy morning we finally had an albacore jig strike. The fish charged the boat, splashing and boiling in the chum line. My six passengers had retreated from the spray-swept, rolling deck to their bunks and were roused with some difficulty. Pale, slack-jawed and buttery-eyed, they came lurching and staggering from the cabin. Frantically I urged them to grab rods and get baits in the water. Those that did were rewarded with instant hookups.

Ready rods were lined up in their holders, but one dazed character asked which one he should use. "Take any one at all," I hollered as I turned to gaff a jig fish. We now had three bait fish going.

After sacking the jig fish, I searched for the questioner to see why he was not yet in action. To my amazement, I found him off in the corner where the passengers had stowed their gear, impaling an anchovy on the opened snap of a large swivel dangling from the tip of a heavy trolling rig. I was dumfounded—the poor boob didn't know a snap swivel from a fish hook!

It was 1938 and a fishing friend and I were catching yellowtail from Schipper's old SAN ANTONIO anchored at the Coronado Islands. Rebaiting our hooks with live sardines we made simultaneous casts, dropping our baits within a couple feet of the same spot. A few seconds later we both had running strikes and set our hooks at the same time. As our lines seemed to converge, we decided to separate in hopes of preventing a tangle. He moved aft along the rail and I moved forward. Pumping hard, we quickly gained control and soon had color on one yellowtail. It appeared that one of us was tangled, but discovered when the fish was gaffed that both our hooks were embedded side by side in the fish's upper jaw, occupying the same hole in the flesh. The poor yellow never had a chance with the pair of us pulling on him from opposite directions. As we had equal claims on the fish, a "corporation" was formed then

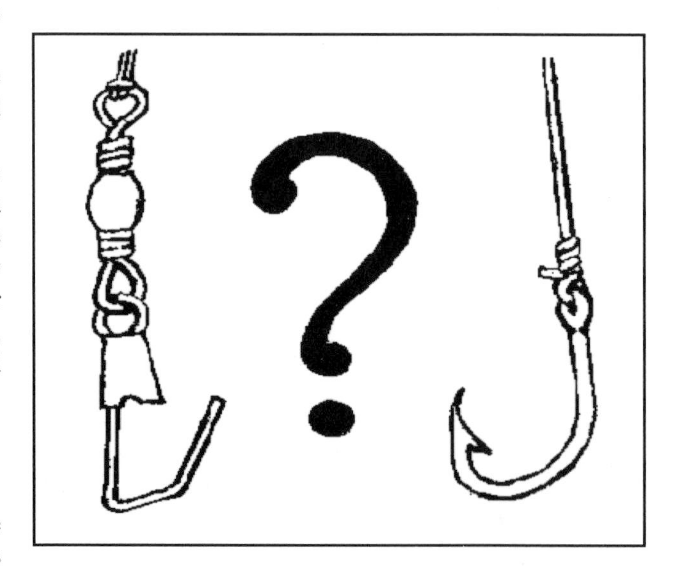

Which is a fishhook?

and there. Our catches were pooled for a 50-50 split of proceeds when sold.

Over the years I've enjoyed wide-open bass fishing on many occasions, but the best rod-and-reel catch of my life was made on June 17, 1947. It was on Earl Strong's CALYPSO running from the Oceanside Pier. My longtime fishing buddy Les had talked me into making the trip from L.A. specifically for bass fishing, a specialty then as now, of Oceanside boats. Les considered himself a bass expert and was very competitive. When fishing with a companion he always insisted on counting the catch and comparing numbers.

Kelp bass, Paralabrax clathratus.

The day began poorly when precious fishing time was wasted waiting for bait. After a couple of hours the bait boat found a few scoops of herring (brown bait). I had not much hope the trip would be worth the journey and the delays. How wrong I was!

After a run down the coast we anchored up in a kelp bed and began fishing. It was a calm, sunny day and the current was ideal, running straight into the weeds. Due to the shortage of bait there was no chumming. It didn't matter. The calicos were absolutely ravenous, several charging a bait the minute it was presented. My long Calcutta bamboo rod was armed with a Penn 155 reel, green braided nylon line and a blue steel leader with 2/0 hook. Every bait resulted in a hookup of a sizeable fish. One sack was filled to capacity and a second was filling fast when the bait ran out. Dead queenfish were scraped from the bottom of the tank and once-used pieces were picked from the deck. Bass continued to bite and, before it disintegrated, I boated three fish on one mangled herring. It was fantastic fishing.

"Let's don't count the fish," blurted Les, much embarrassed by his one-sack catch. Laughing, I reminded him that he always wanted a count. My two sackfuls held 63 bass. Les had managed only 30. It was an exceptional take even for those times. We sold them, as was our custom then, at a San Pedro market. They weighed 186 pounds for which we received $24.18, or 13 cents per pound.

Such bass slaughters are rare these days but fairly common 50 years ago. The general attitude then was to take whatever was legal and sell it. It was a hangover from the Depression days, a type of commercial sportfishing. Seven years later bass were removed from the market and present size and possession limits were imposed.

WHAT'S IN A NAME?

As a youngster learning to fish my interest in every phase of the sport was intense, including the proper identification of the many varieties caught. It was soon apparent that there was considerable confusion about common names. Where closely related species presented only minor external differences to the untrained eye, the muddle was compounded. For instance, the yellowfin croaker and the lowly tomcod, or white croaker, were often mistaken one for the other, as were the three basses and the multitude of rockfish.

So fascinated was I with fish and fishing that I wished at the time to pursue ichthyology as an adult career. There was a recognition handbook printed by the Fish & Game Department, but my first researches into solving identification mysteries were via the massive tomes of Jordan and Evermann, published in 1896. I quickly learned the scientific names of all common marine game fishes, most of which I remember to this day.

Trying to translate the scientific names and determine their relation to the various species became a sort of sideline hobby. It is a very complex system. According to the rules of zoological nomenclature names must be rendered in Latin or Latinized form, but I found that many other languages contribute to the method, including Greek and Japanese, which often makes a translation extremely difficult.

Some names are becoming, colorful or amusing, but many seem wildly inappropriate. Let me present a few examples. To begin with there is the broadbill. Over 2,000 years ago Aristotle knew him as Xiphias. Now defined in Greek and Latin we have *Xiphias gladius*, or "sword swordfish." Known also to the Ancients was *Thunnus*, the bluefin tuna. So *Thunnus thynnus* means "tuna tuna." Exact but not very imaginative. Our esteemed albacore went through several name changes over two centuries from *Germo alalunga* to *Thunnus germo* to the current well-fitting *Thunnus alalunga*, or "long-winged tuna."

Proper, but obscure in translation, are the labels for Pacific salmon. The generic *Oncorhynchus* means "hooksnout," but the various specific names are derived from the Russian vernacular. Try translating those! For the reasonably suitable let's try *Pimelometopon pulchrum*, meaning "beautiful fat forehead." That is fairly good, even flattering, for a sheephead. A lingcod is neither a ling nor a cod but is *Ophiodon elongatus* or "elongated snake-tooth." The sculpin,

Jack Mackerel, Trachurus symmetricus

Scorpaena guttata, is "speckled dorsal spines." Jack mackerel, *Trachurus symmetricus*, is "symmetrical rough tail." Try *Scorpaenichthys marmoratus* or "marbled dorsal-spined fish" for the cabezon. "Goldfish leader" sounds okay for the dolphinfish, *Coryphaena hippurus*. Also good is "California grinder ray" for the bat ray, *Myliobatis californicus*. Acceptable is *Gymnothorax mordax*, meaning "biting naked-breast," for a moray eel. The insignificant rock wrasse bears one of my favorite handles: *Halichoeres semicinctus*, or "half-banded pig-of-the-sea."

Sometimes a species is named in honor of a colleague or after a friend. Thus the cusk eel is *Otophidium taylori*, or "Taylor's ear-snake." How about "Stearns' snorer" for the spotfin croaker, *Roncador stearnsii*, or "Cary's high tail" for the rainbow perch, *Hypsurus caryi*. The southern bluefin of Australian waters is *Thunnus maccoyii*, or "MacCoy's tuna."

Two hundred years ago some boffin saddled the bonito tribe with the ridiculous generic name *Sarda*, meaning "sardine." Thus our local favorite, *Sarda chiliensis*, is a "Chilean sardine." The dogtooth tuna I caught in the Marshall Islands is *Gymnosarda unicolor*, or "one color naked sardine!"

Our most numerous local family are the rockfish of genus *Sebastes*, meaning "magnificent." Don't know how they came up with that one. It would have been fitting for something more impressive like a marlin. Anyway, we have *Sebastes paucispinis*, or "magnificent few spines" for the already misnamed salmon grouper. The Italian bocaccio (big mouth) is a more proper common name. I suppose the "few spines" refers to the somewhat less horny head on this species compared to some of the other rockfishes. The apparent similarity of the olive rockfish to a bass is noted by *Sebastes serranoides*, meaning "magnificent; resembling the *Serranidae* or sea-bass family." The fish is widely and incorrectly known as a johnny bass.

None of this has any practical value when it comes to catching fish, but to those concerned with precise identification of their catches it is useful to know the system.

A maximum load of sardines.

These 29 tons of barracuda were made into chicken feed.

Charter group poses in front of Morris ticket office at Santa Monica, c. 1933. Rent rods on the right.

Above: Some dandy big yellows and tuna on boat SAN ANTONIO. Left: Scotty Lacade poses with fish in front of his Santa Monica ticket office. Competition there was fierce in the late '20s.

So long, fishermen. May you always find exotics under your paddies!

Ed

APPENDIX

CALIFORNIA SPORTFISHING BARGES
EX-SAILING SHIPS

ANNIE M. ROLPH, 4-masted barkentine. Built by Rolph Shipbuilding Corp. at Rolph, CA, 1919. Barge at Newport, Huntington Beach and Malibu c. 1937. Wrecked at Rocky Point 7-26-42.

AURORA, 4-masted barkentine (later schooner), built at Everett Shipbuilding Co., Everett, WA, 1901. In lumber trade for Chas. Nelson Co. Laid up in 1927. Sold to H. J. Cochran in 1932 for barge at Monterey. Possibly at Redondo for a short time. Stranded and lost 1-13-35.

CHARLES BROWN, ex-TOKAI MARU, 2-masted schooner, 87 feet long, built 1904 in Japan for sealing. Probably pinched for poaching. Paper says "once notorious as a Japanese narcotic runner and a 'death ship.'' Used in movies? Owned by Capt. Olaf Olsen and was barge at Santa Monica at least until 1926. Wrecked 4-21-32 at Laguna Beach. Dent E. Paxton and Jack and Ralph Tubbs were co-owners when lost.

ESTHER BUHNE, 3-masted schooner, built by H. Bendixsen at Fairhaven, CA, 1887. Barge at Newport Beach. Wrecked 2-13-27.

FOX, ex-ALLEN A., 3-masted schooner. Built by H. Bendixsen at Fairhaven, CA, 1888. One of Olsen's barges at Santa Monica 1927 to 1942. Station barge at Long Beach during WW II. Abandoned in Mexico 1952.

FULLERTON, 4-masted barkentine, built by Hay & Wright, Alameda 1902. Bought by Hans Monstad 1925. Wrecked at Redondo, 5-7-27.

GEORGE E. BILLINGS, 5-masted schooner, built by Hall Bros., Port Blakely, WA, 1903. Bought for barge at Del Mar in 1926. Bought by Robert Oefinger, moved to Ocean Park in 1930. Burned by her owner as a liability on 2-10-41.

GEORGE U. HIND, 4-masted barkentine, built by Rolph Shipbuilding Co., Rolph, CA, 1919. Under tow from San Diego for barge service at Oceanside 4-3-36 when she became unmanageable in high winds and was driven ashore at Solana Beach. Owner was Harry Levy. Salvaged by Coast Guard and repaired at San Diego. Relocated at Oceanside. Beached 9-15 in sinking condition. Hulk broken up by gale of 12-28-36.

GEORGINA, 4-masted barkentine, built by Bendixsen at Fairhaven, CA, 1901. Bought 1927 by A. J. Larsen for barge at Redondo. Stranded 1935. Salvaged and later scrapped.

GLENDALE, later NEW POINT LOMA, 3-masted schooner, built by Hans Bendixsen, Fairhaven, CA, 1888. Barge at Venice, 1930. Barge for Star & Crescent Boat Co., San Diego, in 1932. Converted to crane barge and lost off Crescent City while under tow of the KANAK on 9-18-50.

GRATIA, steel bark, built at Port Glasgow, Scotland, 1891. Capt. Wm. Storey was owner when wrecked near Rocky Point in gale of 4-20-32. Valued at $10,000. Six crew removed by breaches buoy from cliff at 3 AM.

IRENE, 4-masted schooner, built by H. Bendixsen, Fairhaven, CA, 1900. Owned by Gardiner Mill Co., Gardiner, Oregon until 1920s. Made last voyage in 1926. Movie ship. Barge at Manhattan Beach, 1930s. OwnerA. J. Larsen. W. E. Monstad was owner in 1936. Sank near Redondo 1-28-37.

JAMES MCKENNA, 2-masted scow schooner, Long Beach and Seal Beach 1925 to postwar. Fate unknown.

JAMES TUFT, 4-masted barkentine, built by Hall Bros., Port Blakely, WA, 1901. Sold by George E. Billings 5-8-28 to Claude Cummings of Los Angeles. Fishing barge in 1931, owned by Fred O. Henderson. Later burned as gambling barge CASINO at Long Beach 8-22-35.

JANE L. STANFORD, 4-masted barkentine,built by H. Bendixsen, Fairhaven, CA, 1892. Sold in 1926 by Robert Dollar to Charles McCarthy. Briefly at Redondo, moved to Ventura and Santa Barbara. Run down by steamer HUMBOLDT on 8-30-29. Remains blown up at Santa Rosa Island.

KOHALA, 4-masted barkentine, built by H. Bendixsen at Fairhaven, CA, in 1901. Barge at Redondo in 1928. Mistakenly sunk by U.S. bombers 12-25-41.

LAHAINA, 4-masted barkentine, built by W.A. Boole in Oakland, CA, 1901. Bought by Hans Monstad inAug. 1925. Barge at Redondo and Hermosa. Wrecked 9-25-33 at Pt. Vicente.

LAZY DAZE, ex-RADIO, 2-masted schooner. Postwar barge at Oceanside. Owned by Herb Poole. Burned 5-9-53.

MARGARET C., 2-masted schooner. Off Redondo 1922-23? Possible first ship barge. Later a derelict in Catalina Harbor after movie work. Historian Bill Olesen writes she was "a rare example of the round-bilged sharp-bowed S.F. Bay schooner which must have flaunted her shape among the many scow contemporaries during her heyday."

MARY LOU, ex-MARION G. DOUGLAS, 3-masted schooner built at Fox River, N. S., 1917. May have been barge at San Clemente, 1930. Possibly used as tuna transport for Halfhill Packing Co. of Long Beach. Beached on seaward side of Terminal Island and later burned for a Harbor Day celebration c. 1938.

MELROSE, 4-masted schooner, built by Hitchings & Joyce, Hoquiam, WA, 1902. At Newport and Long Beach, 1930s, San Clemente 1937. Capt. Klebingat had her and one of Morris brothers as 2nd Mate, c. 1920, while in lumber trade. Beached seaward sideTerminal Island and later burned. Not to be confused with sidewheel ferry, MELROSE (see next page).

MINDANAO, ex-CALIFORNIA, ex-ANDY MAHONY, 4 -masted schooner. Built by J. Lindstrom at Aberdeen, WA, 1902. Barge at Venice and Newport Beach 1930 to 1941. Owned by C. E. McFarland. Burned by city government as a liability 5-28-46.

MINNIE A. CAINE, 4-masted schooner built by Moran Bros. at Seattle, WA, 1900. Capt. Olaf Olsen's pride and joy. Wrecked at foot of Sunset Blvd, Santa Monica 9-24-39.

MONTEZUMA, 2 masted scow schooner. Barge at Long Beach, 1925. Fate unknown.

MURIEL, 4-masted schooner, built by Hay & Wright, Alameda, CA, 1895. Sold to Frank Lloyd of movies in 1923. Owned by Rube Shafer when wrecked at Balboa, CA, 7-3-25, on way to barge service.

NARWHAL, steam whaling bark, built by Dickie Bros., San Francisco, CA, 1883. Olaf Olsen bought her from Allen Knight in March 1925. Moored off Santa Monica, but standing masts caused excessive rolling. Sold for movie work. Beached in south San Diego Bay and burned, 1934.

OCEANIA VANCE, 3-masted schooner, built by Hall Bros., Port Blakely, WA, 1888. Served briefly as a tuna transport. Became a Monstad barge in 1935 and was wrecked at Topaz St, Redondo, 3-25-36.

OLYMPIC, 4-masted barkentine, built at Bath, ME, 1892. Bought by Capt. J. M. Andersen. Barge at Hermosa Beach from 1926 until laid up c.1935, later scrapped. Replaced by OLYMPIC II.

OLYMPIC II, ex-STAR OF FRANCE, iron ship, built Belfast, Ireland, 1877. Bought by Capt. J. M. Andersen, March 1934, as replacement for worn-out OLYMPIC. Rammed and sunk by Japanese steamer SAKITO MARU near San Pedro, 9-4-40.

RAINBOW, ex-MAKAWELI, 4-masted barkentine, 899 tons, built by W.A. Boole & Son, Oakland, CA, 1902. Barge at Long Beach, 8-15-35.

SAMAR, 4-masted schooner. Built by Hay & Wright at Alameda, CA, 1901. Bought by Joe Guion in 1931. Used for movie work and as fishing barge at Catalina, 1932-34. Barge at Long Beach, 1937-38, owned by George McIntyre. Converted to floating machine shop during war. Aground in Mexico 1952.

SANTA CLARA, ship, built at Bath, ME, 1876. Barge at San Pedro. Owned by H. Carstensen. Sold to R. Biblehouse 1931, and extensively modified for movie work. Sank in Cerritos Channel 1939, raised and sunk at sea 1950s.

SHAMROCK, ex-INDIANA, ship, built by E. & A. Sewell at Bath, ME, 1876. Barge at Long Beach in 1930s.

STAR OF SCOTLAND, ex-KENILWORTH, steel 4-masted bark, built at Port Glasgow, Scotland, 1887. Bought by Charles Arnold 1930. Off Santa Monica 1930-38. Sold to Tony Cornero and converted to gambling barge REX. Bought by Frank Hellenthal and converted to 6-masted schooner, 1941. Sunk by German submarine in South Atlantic 11-13-42.

THOMAS P. EMIGH, 4-masted barkentine, built Tacoma Shipbuilding Co., Tacoma, WA, 1901. Sold by Charles Nelson Co. 5-21-27 to S. F. Monstad of Redondo. Wrecked in 65 m.p.h. gale at Redondo 4-20-32. W. L. Monstad valued EMIGH at $16,000.

VIRGINIA A., 2-masted Chesapeake Bay schooner. Barge at Malibu, 1938. Owned by Al Camp and Earl Gray.

WILLIAM BOWDEN, 4-masted schooner, built by Hall Bros., Port Blakely, WA, 1892. Bought by Hans Carstensen and A.R. Paulsen, 7-31-25. Wrecked at Redondo 2-12-26.

After the storm: WILLIAM BOWDEN beached at Redondo in January, 1926.

BARGES, MISCELLANEOUS HULL TYPES

Code:
F Flat, rectangular scow barge
S Ex-steam or motor vessel (tugs, cargo ships, etc.)
L Ex-naval landing craft
U Unknown
P Postwar (WW II) Exact dates unknown.

Name	Type	Location	Operational Dates
ACE I	L	Dana Point.	P
AILEEN	U	Redondo	1930s
ANNIE B.	F	Seal Beach, inside breakwater	1982
BACCHUS	U	Venice	1926
BAITWELL	F	Catalina, Ocean Park	1930s
THE BARGE	U	Newport Beach	1930s
BAY	F	San Pedro inside breakwater	P
BILL'S BARGE, ex-CHALLENGER	U	Redondo, Huntington Beach	1920s
CHALLENGER II	U	Redondo	1923
BLUE SEA	S	Long Beach	1928
BONNIE K.	U	Redondo	U
BOUNTY	S	Long Beach, Monterey	1930s
BUCCANEER	S	Paradise Cove, Redondo.	P
C-1	F	Venice	1936-38?
CALIFORNIA	S	Redondo	1957
DIXIE	L	Newport Beach	1950s
EARL WOOD'S BARGE	F	Catalina	1925-31
ELSIE I	F	Huntington Beach	1951
ELSIE II	F	Huntington Beach	P
EMPEROR	S	Redondo	1938
EMPRESS	S	Catalina	1936-40
FRANK LAWRENCE	F	Cabrillo Beach	P
F. S. LOOP	S	Seal Beach	1939-40
GANDER	S	Newport Beach	P
GEORGIA	S	Newport Beach	P
GLENN MAYNE	S	Oceanside	1938-41
HEMLOCK	F	Long Beach, inside breakwater	1948
HIPPOGLOSSUS	F	Malibu	1938
HOMER	S	Seal Beach	1939-40
HUNTINGTON BARGE	F	Huntington Beach	1930s
IKE WALTON	F	San Diego	1926-?
ISLE OF REDONDO	F	Redondo	1980-present
IWO JIMA, (See TRADEWINDS)	L	Newport Beach	P
KILROY	U	Belmont Pier	1947
LADY LUCK	U	Paradise Cove	P
LIGHTHOUSE	F	San Pedro, inside breakwater	P
MAGDALENA BAY, ex-PANAMA	S	Hermosa	1936-38
MANANA	L	Redondo	P
MC CULLAH BROS. #3	F	Newport Beach	P
MELROSE	S	Redondo	1932
NEPTUNE	U	Huntington Beach	P
NEW BOUNTY, ex-MARTHA BUEHNER	S	L. Beach Pierpoint	1947
NEW RAINBOW	U	Belmont Pier	1947
NO-NAME	F	Santa Barbara	1954-56
NORTH WIND	U	Santa Monica	1943-53

Name	Type	Location	Operational Dates
PARADISE	U	Paradise Cove	P
PARAMOUNT	S	Newport Beach	1936
PIERPOINT QUEEN	S	Long Beach, inside breakwater	1948
POINT LOMA	S	Redondo, San Diego	1927-30
OCEAN	F	San Pedro inside bkwtr	1938
OCEANSIDE	U	Oceanside	1934
PAPROCA	F	Long Beach	1921-24
PT. MUGU I	F	Pt. Mugu	1930s
PT. MUGU II	F	Pt. Mugu	1930s
RETRIEVER	S	Redondo	1950s
RICH RICHIE	F	Cabrillo Beach	P
SACRAMENTO	S	Redondo	1953
SAN WAN	S	Santa Barbara	1941
SEA BREEZE	F	San Pedro	P
SEA COASTER	T	San Pedro	1958
SEA WITCH	U	Redondo	1939
SIERRA, ex-VIRGINIA OLSON	S	Whites Point	1930s
STAR OF SCOTLAND, ex-TEXAS	S	Santa Monica	1941-42
SWALLOW	U	Huntington Beach	P
TRADEWINDS, ex-IWO JIMA	L	Santa Monica, Laguna	1946
VARGA	S	Huntington Beach	P

A side gallery on STAR OF SCOTLAND.

Jackpolling a mackerel on a barge.

BIBLIOGRAPHY

California Dept. of Fish & Game, *various publications: Fish Bulletins, Report of the Commissioners, 1916, Calif. Fish & Game, Outdoor California.*

Cannon, Raymond, *How to Fish the Pacific Coast*, Menlo Park, CA 1953

Chapman, Wilbert M., *Fishing in Troubled Waters*, N.Y. 1949.

City of Redondo Beach, *archival material*

Davis, J. Charles 2nd, *California Saltwater Fishing*, N.Y. 1949

Eisenberg, Lee and Taylor, DeCourcy, *The Ultimate Fishing Book*, Boston 1981.

Farrington, S. Kip Jr., *Pacific Game Fishing,*
Fishing the Pacific, Offshore and On, N.Y. 1942, 1953.

Grey, Zane, *Tales of Fishes,*
Tales of Fishing Virgin Seas,
Tales of Swordfish and Tuna,
Tales of the Anglers Eldorado,
Tales of Tahitian Waters. N.Y. 1919-1931

Griswold, F. Grey, *Some Fish and Fishing*

Heilner,Van Campen, *Salt Water Fishing,* Philadelphia 1937.

Holder, Charles Frederick *The Log of a Sea Angler,*
Big Game at Sea,
The Channel Islands of California, Boston, 1906, 1908, 1910.

Jordan, David Starr and Evermann, Barton W., *American Food and Game Fishes,* N.Y. 1922

La Monte, Francesca, *North American Game Fishes,*
Marine Game Fishes of the World, N.Y. 1945, 1952.

Major, Harlan, *Salt Water Fishing Tackle*, N.Y. 1939.

Mascarenhas, Capt. Anthony, *Various papers for the Portuguese Historical Society,* San Diego

McClane, A.J., *McClane's Standard Fishing Encyclopedia*, N.Y. 1974

McMillan, Hugh, *Beach Rat Days, Beach Rat Pix*, Newport Beach, 1973.

McMurray, Les, *Fishing Facts Annual, 1946*

Pacific Fisherman, *(magazine) various articles*, Seattle, 1910-1950

Reiger, George, *Profiles in Saltwater Angling,*
Zane Grey, Outdoorsman, N.J., 1973, 1972

Scripps Institute of Oceanography, *various publications.*

Soltesz, Edward, *Pole Fishing for Tuna,* Journal of the San Diego Historical Society, Summer 1991

Thomas, George C., Jr. and Thomas, George C, III, *Game Fish of the Pacific,* Philadelphia, 1930.

Trench, Charles Chenevix, *A History of Angling*, N.Y. 1974

U.S. Fish and Wildlife Service, *various publications.*

University of California Press, *Marine Game Fishes of the Pacific Coast,*

Waterman, Charles F., *Fishing in America, N.Y. 1975.*

Wick, Carl I., *Ocean Harvest, Seattle 1946*

Clippings and stories from the following newspapers, culled from many sources:

Long Beach Press-Telegram
Los Angeles Daily News
Los Angeles Examiner
Los Angeles Harold Express
Los Angeles Record
Los Angeles Times
Los Angeles Tribune
Redondo Daily Breeze
Redondo Reflex
San Diego Tribune
San Diego Union
Santa Monica Evening Outlook

GLOSSARY

Through conversation with some of my younger friends I am aware that much of the fishing lingo used in the Old Days is no longer current. Along with other aspects of the sport, terminology and slang have also changed. Perhaps it may be well to record a few bits of it before it is lost beyond recall. Some of the nomenclature endures today as it was 50, and more, years ago, but often on a regional basis. For example: a word or phrase heard around Morro Bay or Malibu may be unknown in San Diego. Most of the terms below will be familiar to anglers who were fishing more than 30 years ago. Herewith a random and very incomplete sample glossary:

Alligator: Large barracuda.
Army blanket: Large halibut.
Bakelite: The first synthetic resin plastic, invented in 1909. Black or brown in color, it was widely used for sideplates, replacing the hard rubber found on quality reels since the turn of the century. It was very brittle.
Barn door: Large halibut.
Barracuda bird: Tern.
Belinda cod: Widow rockfish.
Blondie: Sardine version of a greenback anchovy. With all scales intact, a healthy sardine appears lighter and more yellowish in color
Blue cod: Cabezon.
Blue streak: Large, lively anchovy, a good hook bait.
Bohunk: The largest size sardine, over 10 inches.
Bonehead: Bonito
Bosco: Starry, honeycomb or bronzespot rockfish.
Counter: Legal sized, commercially marketable fish. In the Old Days there were no size limits on sport caught fish.
Color spot: The dark area seen in clear water that revealed a bait school to a lookout.
Cuttyhunk: Generic name for cable-laid linen fish line.
Darb: Slang superlative for fish of exceptional size or beauty. Sometimes applied to human females.
Ding-ding: A device attached to a pole or rope that was plunged up and down from the stern of a bait boat to frighten surrounded fish towards the center of the net. Until the wings of the net were aboard, an escape route under the boat was open. Sometimes called a scare-crow, or just plain scare.
Feather Merchants: Term applied to fishermen who specialized in casting small feather jigs for barracuda.
Feeler: Handline used for rockfishing in deep water. Often buoyed off to mark a hotspot of biting fish.
Flip: The tiny surface splash, like a raindrop, made by an anchovy. Easily visible in calm water, flips revealed anchovy schools to searching bait boats.
Fluke: Slang name for halibut.
Frog: Mackerel.
German silver: Nickel-zinc alloy used to plate exposed reel parts that are now anodized or chromed.
Goat: Sheephead.
Grumpy: Any rockfish. Now most often applied to bull sand bass.
Helldiver: Cormorant.
Herring: Queenfish, *Seriphus politus,* now called brown bait.
Hueneme: Large anchovy, named for an area believed to be home to bait fish of exceptional size.
Individual: Small kelp or sand bass ten to twelve inches long. Sold in restaurants as "individual rock bass."
Laguna Tuna: Derisive term for bonito or mackerel.
Lampara: Type of hand pulled round-haul net used to catch live bait or any small market fish.

Using a rope gaff on a barge.

Low Bridge: Warning hollered by anglers preparing to cast.

Monterey: Generic name for the clipper-bowed, double-ended hook-and-line market fishing boats found in every California port between the world wars. Descendant of a sail-powered design introduced by Italian immigrants. Built in large numbers at Monterey boatyards. Usually crewed by one to three fishermen. Not many of these seaworthy classics survive today.

Pinback: Spiny dogfish, *Squalus acanthis*. Once sought by set line fishermen for their livers. Now the object of renewed interest by the fish and chips trade.

Pinhead: Tiny bait fish. Also an unpaid helper on a sport boat. Usually a teenage boy eager to earn a deckhand job.

Plunger: Sportboat passenger of limited fishing skill and a predilection for digging in the bait tank.

Pop-belly: Rockfish.

Preo: Percentage, or extra money above wages derived from tips or sale of fish by boat crews.

Racehorse: Large, active sardine; once the favored bait for all game fish.

Rope gaff: Used by pier and barge fishermen to haul up fish too large to bounce. A large treble hook imbedded in a lead weight attached to a rope.

Scarecrow: See ding-ding.

Scoop boat: Vessel engaged in mackerel fishing with handheld dip nets.

Scooter: Barracuda.

Scrub: Small rockfish.

Sea trout: Young white seabass, once caught in large numbers from the numerous piers along the coast, especially at night.

Set line: Long horizontal line supporting several hundred hooks on short leaders, anchored and buoyed at the ends. Widely used for halibut and bottom fish in the Old Days, but rarely seen now. Newport Beach dory fishermen still work this gear.

Sidewinder: Simplest and cheapest form of wooden or metal single action reel, common for pier fishing.

Slimey: Slang term for bocaccio or salmon grouper, *Sebastes paucispinis*.

Snake: Barracuda.

Stovepipe: Large barracuda.

Stinger: Bat ray.

Striker: Weighted barbless hook dressed with feathers used in commercial pole fishing for tuna, bonito, mackerel and barracuda. Now more commonly and confusingly called a "squid."

Sugar bass: Kelp rockfish, *Sebastes atrovirens*. Sometimes applied to olive rockfish.

Water haul: Unproductive set with a bait net. Often the result of a "blind haul" when the net was set without a surface indication of bait fish.

Santa Monica Pier from the newly constructed breakwater, 1934.